LOST AND FOUND
IN SPAIN

LOST AND FOUND IN SPAIN

Tales of an Ambassador's Wife

SUSAN LEWIS SOLOMONT

Austin   New York

This book is memoir. It reflects the author's present recollections of experiences over time. Some names and characteristics have been changed, some events have been compressed, and some dialogue has been recreated.

Published by Disruption Books
Austin, TX, and New York, NY
www.disruptionbooks.com

Distributed by Disruption Books

For ordering information or special discounts for bulk purchases, please contact Disruption Books at info@disruptionbooks.com.

Print ISBN: 978-1-63331-030-8
eBook ISBN: 978-1-63331-031-5

First Edition

To Alan, mi esposo, mi embajador,
our life together is wonderful journey.

To Becca and Stephanie,
thank you for sharing the joy of our adventure,
los quiero mucho a todos.

To Stella Blu, eres una perrita maravillosa.

And to all of us who want
to make a difference in the world.

CONTENTS

FROM BOSTON
TO THE LAND OF OZ

T HE DAY THE WHITE HOUSE called, it was my husband who answered the phone. After a period of silence and the occasional "Yes," "No," and "Of course," I heard Alan exclaim: "Spain? Of course, Spain! We'd love to serve in Spain. I love Spain!" I steadied myself on the wall, unable to believe this sudden change in our destiny.

It was January 2009, three months after the election of President Barack Obama. Alan had worked hard on Obama's campaign, sharing his message of hope and change to new friends and potential donors throughout the country. Recognizing my husband's efforts during the campaign, the new administration's transition team asked whether Alan would be willing to serve as an ambassador. He said yes, but neither of us counted on him actually receiving an overseas appointment. Now he had, and in twelve months' time, we would be trading our home in Weston, Massachusetts, for the US embassy in Spain. We were going to Madrid.

But not so fast . . .

Amid the swell of emotions in the months that followed, I was unable to think very clearly about the impact a three-year foreign service assignment might have on me or on my career. I had worked for over thirty years in the nonprofit world, fundraising for organizations I admired (such as PBS), and helping corporations and foundations make strategic philanthropic decisions. What about my senior position at The Philanthropic Initiative (TPI), a global consulting firm? What about my involvement on the boards of such organizations as the Citi Performing Arts Center (now the Boch Center), the New England Aquarium, and The Commonwealth Institute? I would soon be putting those responsibilities on hold.

Yet I vaguely supposed living in Europe would be stimulating for me. Professionally, I'd gain exposure to European philanthropy and perhaps make new business contacts. I imagined my job would serve as something of an anchor for the rest of my life in Spain—a defining part of me, as it always has been. Even when my two daughters were little, I would leave for work each day while other moms went off to play tennis. Staying at home while my husband worked was the furthest thing from my mind.

Imagine my disbelief, then, when I heard that I *wouldn't* be working in Spain.

In July 2009, Alan and I ventured to Washington, DC, to participate in "ambassador school"—the Department of State's mandatory Ambassadorial Seminar, also lovingly referred to as "charm school." Rest assured, as interesting as this experience was, there was nothing charming about it.

First of all, it was long and grueling. Twelve ambassador designates and their spouses met from eight thirty in the morning to six in the evening, Monday through Friday, for two weeks. Government officials filtered through the room, briefing us about their agencies and the roles we would play abroad. As they introduced us to what increasingly felt like alphabet soup—CIA, DOS, RSO, FBI—I threw myself into the curriculum, taking copious notes and trying to keep all the agencies and their various functions straight. It was like being in college again, subjected to a rigorous immersion in the workings of the government, both in our nation's capital and in our embassies, consulates, and diplomatic missions around the world.

We learned about how to move to our countries, the structure of an embassy, security protocols, and other logistics. We brushed up on the basics of Spain's government and economy, understanding that Spain is a parliamentary democracy and Europe's fifth most powerful and populous country. We learned that Spain is divided into seventeen autonomous communities analogous to America's states. And we learned that Spain's economy—the world's ninth-largest then—was heading toward a terrible recession caused by overdevelopment in the real estate sector and overextension by the banking industry.

The seminar's opening days were fascinating and educational, but also nerve-wracking. The idea of moving abroad and representing the United States in Spain was becoming real. And the experience became even more real—alarmingly real—when the words *conflict of interest* popped up in one conversation with a government official, as in, "Jobs for spouses of ambassadors are often deemed to represent a *conflict of interest.*"

That's right: according to the Department of State, the risk exists that ambassadors might use their official position to benefit a spouse's employer or client. So the government not only didn't want me working, but also requested that I give up my seats on the boards and foundations I served and from which I derived great satisfaction.

At least I would be exchanging my professional commitments for meaningful work at the embassy, right? Actually, that wasn't necessarily the case, either. My first inkling of the diminutive role of "ambassador's spouse" came when our instructors circulated to each participant a loose-leaf binder with important information and resources, including the résumé and curriculum vitae of every ambassador present. I was immediately struck by the realization that the binder's contents excluded any pertinent information about any of the ambassadors' spouses. A bit vexed, I began to wonder what Secretary of State Hillary Clinton—the most powerful woman in the United States at that time, and certainly the most famous political spouse—would say. Surely she wouldn't approve of this glaring omission!

As I learned more about what was expected of an ambassador's spouse, I came to hope that perhaps I *could* still "work" by doing something important for our nation's embassy in Madrid. I met a previous ambassador's wife who had been a journalist for many leading newspapers and institutions. While residing in her host country, she would organize intimate lunches with journalists and have conversations focused on important issues of the day. Her embassy loved those gatherings and was thrilled that she organized and ran them. Her skills and expertise were highly valued and deeply respected. Upon hearing this, I imagined organizing meaningful events that would help the United States and our embassy in Spain accomplish important objectives. It wouldn't be a job in the conventional sense, but I could live with it. Ultimately, I had to find meaning and value in whatever I ended up doing.

When we arrived in Spain in January 2010, I went around to every department or "section," as they are known in embassies, and offered my services. The embassy staff were all very polite. They smiled and promised they would call me. But they didn't. To them, I was very much "the spouse" in the traditional sense; my job was to stand-and-smile and support the ambassador.

I took this rejection to heart. *How could nobody want me?* I thought. *I'm good! I'm smart! I'm capable!*

I told myself that it wasn't personal, that these workers were busy with their demanding jobs. But I couldn't deny that receiving the brush-off was frustrating and incomprehensible. Everyone in the foreign service—from the ambassador, whose official title included the phrase *Extraordinary and Plenipotentiary*, down to the interns—had an important role to play. Yet there I was, little more than an accessory to my husband, with no official role and of seemingly little professional value to the embassy.

One thing about me: I'm relentless. I'm not the type to just let things be. Acquiescence is not in my DNA. If there wasn't a meaningful role for me to fill—something that would allow me to put my own skills and intelligence to work—then I would create one. I didn't want to simply be "the ambassador's wife." I wanted to be Susan Solomont.

Given my background in charitable causes, I began by convening groups of philanthropists. Working with a protocol team (the people in the embassy who know and reach out to the local community), we helped identify leaders in Spanish philanthropy and considered what they were doing. We then organized a roundtable discussion of about thirty-five people. To make this happen, I had to convince some of the embassy's sections that it was a worthwhile endeavor.

And I had to get it funded, because money doesn't just appear for these things.

And I had to make sure people would come. This was the easiest part—an invitation from the United States embassy is a powerful draw.

And I had to convince the embassy employees, the foreign service officers, that I could pull the whole thing off.

Getting departments to engage with me about a roundtable discussion wasn't easy. I think they finally said, "Let's just let her do it and see what happens."

I continued on like this for months, seeking out and scrapping together opportunities to contribute my skills and talents, buoyed by my husband's constant support and encouragement. "If this adventure doesn't work for one of us," he would say, "it doesn't work for either of us." It took nearly a year to create a role for myself: helping launch initiatives and mold programs in which I believed.

My main interest became women in business. I strove to shine a light on what Spanish women were doing, what American women were doing, and how we could all help one another. I discovered that hardly any networking opportunities existed for Spanish women, even though a significant number of them served in senior leadership roles in Spanish businesses. I found common ground with a female embassy employee who shared my interest and had a professional stake in meeting Spanish business leaders, and together we launched a networking program called the Women's Leadership Series. It became a great success and featured programs such as "Women in Journalism" and "Women in Social Media and Marketing." Channeling my inner Oprah, I served as moderator, asking participants about their paths to success. I became more visible in the community and soon began receiving requests to speak and give magazine and newspaper interviews. I was developing my own voice, making a difference, and loving every minute of it.

We have heard a lot about the need for women to "lean in" to their careers. Throughout my life, work always defined who I was. I never needed any encouragement to make the most out of every career or professional opportunity that came my way. But when Alan became an ambassador, I had to shift my frame of reference and make the best of a series of opportunities outside of what I had considered my "career" to that point. What I learned during my time in Spain is that it is possible to recreate one's assigned role—and to reinvent one's career in the process.

I believe in seizing opportunities, even when we don't really know how they will turn out. With openness and a willingness to experiment, not to mention persistence and a little hard work, we can make any situation our own. That's just as true for me as it would be for the wife of a soldier assigned to a new base clear across the country, for the husband of a woman who has just been named CEO, or for anyone seeking a new identity or voice. Whatever your new reality is, you can play second fiddle—and yet not be second fiddle. If *spouse* doesn't really capture this new, more complex way of being, then we need to create a new name for it.

This book describes my efforts to find a new identity for myself, and recounts the joy and power I experienced while finding my voice. It began as a series of letters I wrote to friends and family back in the United States to keep them posted about our activities in Spain. Initially, these letters (I called each one *Hola*, the Spanish word for "hello") had a readership of precisely thirteen friends. As time passed, more and more people asked to receive these Holas—and gave them rave reviews. Like me, readers were swept along by the adventure of it all. They wanted to experience our time in Spain vicariously through the letters. By the end of our tour, some three thousand people were receiving an Hola from me every month or so. The letters also were published on the embassy's official website, in both English and Spanish.

When I completed my final Hola and returned to the United States, many readers asked me to turn my letters into a book. Although the idea of writing a book struck me as uncomfortable, I tentatively asked the advice of a few experts, including literary agent Helen Rees, writer and editor Seth Schulman, and a few authors at Grub Street, an organization designed to help writers. Everyone who reviewed my letters agreed on one thing: my thirty-four Holas did not amount to a full-length book. But after a lot of convincing, my readers and friends persuaded me to transform these letters into something similar: a personal memoir.

I undertook this labor with a great deal of reluctance. While my time in Spain was exhilarating, life-changing, and frustrating, I still wasn't sure it was worthy of publication. I ultimately decided to work through my personal discomfort and tell my story because I suspected that others might find some value in it. Let me be clear: this value, should it exist, does not derive from my own exceptionality. I am not a jet-setting diplomat, either by training or by inclination. I'm an ordinary person who was thrust into some extraordinary circumstances, and who was fortunate enough to do and learn some amazing things in the process.

I also wrote this memoir to offer an inside look into my improbable adventure, to reveal some of the nuts and bolts of America's foreign service, and to dispel some popular misconceptions about what it means to serve as a diplomat abroad. I want readers to understand what an embassy is and how it functions; what ambassadors do and what goes on behind the scenes; and why diplomatic work is so important in today's complex world.

Many people assume that an ambassador's job is glamorous, with days spent traveling the country and attending social teas and fancy dinner parties. That is a myth. True, the job involves travel and has its exciting aspects, which I touch on in the following chapters. In some ways, landing in Spain felt similar to Dorothy's adventure in the magical land of Oz. But serving as ambassador is hard work. Every day is scheduled from morning to night, balancing invitations, requests, and needs from government agencies, industry leaders, and cultural institutions.

Early on, I also learned that you're not just the ambassador to the capital city—you're the ambassador to the entire country. This book reflects that exhausting reality, touching on the treasures to be found throughout the entire country of Spain. Traveling through Spain allowed us to experience the country's food, art, cultural institutions, and beauty. We met people in Spanish cities, towns, and villages, seizing every opportunity that arose and trying to make a positive impact.

As I've intimated, another thing I learned is that the US Department of State hasn't kept up with cultural changes to the meaning of *spouse*. Multinational companies and the foreign services of other countries offer spouses compensation along with explicit roles to fulfill during assignments abroad. Yet as the wife of an American ambassador to Spain, I was only a "trailing spouse," with no compensation or prescribed set of duties. The personal journey on which I embarked—to craft a meaningful role for myself as "the ambassador's wife"—was born of frustration, loneliness, and a dogged determination to do something valuable while abroad. Had the State Department been more progressive in its dealings with spouses, my experience in Spain might have been much different.

Ultimately, I believe my journey illustrates what's possible for all of us in life. After my time in Spain, I can tell you that a middle-aged woman can uproot herself from her comfortable existence and find her way. We often hear about the "gig economy" and how people's lives are no longer set in stone, where they take one job, stay with it their entire life, and then retire. Instead, people now embark on many different jobs and career paths, sometimes simultaneously, and in no set order. These days, *retirement*—a word I strongly dislike—often is just another word for a life change. My experience as recounted in this book thus reflects what is happening to millions of men and women across the country and the world. My personal story demonstrates that even after enjoying a career that has defined your entire life, you can embark on a fresh and fulfilling path. This is true even when you occupy a status with no salary, role, or concrete set of expectations.

In keeping with the original spirit of the Holas, I've written these chapters as a series of connected essays rather than proceeding in strict chronological order. This allows me to capture my experience from different angles, exploring topics like local culture, food, and religion, while depicting my adaptation or reinvention of the role of diplomatic spouse. The result, I hope, is part travelogue, part personal history, and part manifesto on the possibilities of twenty-first-century career and spousal roles.

Writing this book has been an exercise in memory and reflection, a chance to give meaning to a key phase of my life. Now that I'm back home, I'm a different person from who I was. I know that, and I'm glad for it. I've become much clearer on what I want—and don't want. I've become better at paying more attention to what I agree to take on, and to saying no when necessary. That's not to say I have everything figured out. Not at all. I still feel as though I'm on an incredible journey that I piece together slowly, each and every day. Some people know exactly where they want to go and what they want to do. Or at least they say they do. Well, I don't. But I do know this: I am not the type to sit quietly by as an appendage to someone else. That's just not me.

There's this joke, which may not be politically correct, about a little boy who comes home from school really excited one day. He shouts, "Mommy, Mommy, Mommy! I'm going to be in the school play!"

"Great, honey," she replies. "What are you going to be?"

"I'm going to play the father!"

And his mother says, "You march yourself right back inside, and you tell that teacher you want a speaking part!"

I, too, want a speaking part. I always have. And I always will.

ONE

"DARLIN', DO NOT FEAR WHAT YOU DON'T REALLY KNOW"

"**A**RE YOU READY FOR THIS?" my husband asked, eyebrows raised, as the airplane touched down in Madrid. It was seven thirty on the morning of January 9, 2010. Our family of four plus our dog, Stella Blu (she flew in baggage), had spent the past eight hours hurtling toward our new life in Spain. We didn't know what to expect, but we all knew something important was about to unfold.

I caught Alan's gaze, somewhat more awake and alert now thanks to the coffee and croissants served by the flight attendants. I knew what my husband wanted to hear, and for his sake, I was pleased to say it: "Showtime."

As the plane taxied and came to a halt, the passengers stood up, stretching their weary limbs and grabbing their carry-ons. The four of us—our daughter Stephanie in the seat next to me, Alan, and our daughter Becca across the aisle—enjoyed a final, brief moment of connection that I'll always remember. For better or for worse, we were in it together.

An hour earlier, I had awoken just before my alarm went off, as if it were just another day. My eyes cracked open and adjusted to the plane's dim lighting. We had a big day ahead of us, one of the biggest of our lives. Like most people on a long flight, we had boarded the plane in jeans, leggings, and comfy shirts and sweaters, but given what was in store for us, we would be wearing much different clothing when we stepped off.

I nudged Stephanie in an effort to wake her. She barely flinched. It's not easy to wake an eighteen-year-old long before the sun, let alone when she's slept for only a few hours. I jostled her arm back and forth until her eyelids parted. "Hey," I whispered. "It's time."

She rubbed her blond hair from her face and stretched her lanky arms and legs. "Really, Mom? Leave me alone. I'm *so* tired."

"Really, Steph."

I woke the others, eliciting a similar reaction from Becca. Then I slid from my seat and dragged myself to the front of the plane. Nobody noticed me sidestep down the center aisle, carrying my clean clothes and makeup bag. Most passengers were asleep, their faces hidden behind blankets. The lavatory was vacant. I clicked the lock shut and looked into the mirror. *Okay,* I thought. *Let's do this.*

Working as quickly as I could while crammed into such a tiny space, I eased out of my leggings and T-shirt, and shook and stretched myself into an elegant black dress. I had to sit down and contort my body in order to wrestle on my pantyhose and Spanx (yes, I was wearing those, too!). Having accomplished these acrobatics, I topped off the outfit with a pair of black suede Manolo Blahniks and a few understated bracelets. I had given careful thought to what I would wear today and to the image I wanted to deliver: professionalism, elegance, stylishness, but *not* flashiness.

I brushed my teeth, careful not to drink the water (which, according to the sign, was *no potable*). Next, I ran a brush through my hair—it didn't need much, thanks to my blowout in Boston the day before. When I had finished applying foundation, eye shadow, and lipstick, I looked okay for someone who had just taken a transatlantic, red-eye flight. I was going for a classic, elegant look—like an executive on Madison Avenue setting off to an early evening cocktail reception, ready for anything.

Inside, however, I was feeling the opposite: numb and nervous, not entirely conscious of what was happening. What was in store for me here?

I'm not the type to move around a lot. When I arrive at a place, I tend to stay. I grew up in Brooklyn, New York, and lived on the same street, in the same house, until I was eighteen. The day my parents moved, I sat on the floor of our old living room sobbing while movers evacuated our furniture piece by piece. I remember announcing that the "new house" would never truly feel like home to me. And it never did.

I found a second home in the Boston area, where I moved in 1979 after graduating college. In those thirty-plus years in Boston, I lived in four different places: an apartment in Brookline; an apartment on Boston's waterfront; our first home in Weston; and the home in which we currently live. Each of those moves felt exciting in its own way. I knew that this time around, moving to Spain, I had embarked on the adventure of a lifetime. People never stopped telling me so. Yet I could not feel the excitement.

Three and a half years was a long time to spend abroad, without family and friends, speaking a foreign language, living in a home that was not our own—a *very* long time. The plane hadn't even landed, and I was homesick already.

I ran my hands down the front of my black dress and adjusted a pin I had attached (some might call it a brooch, but that sounds like something my grandmother would wear). Giving myself one last, anxious look in the mirror, I took a deep breath and returned to my seat. "Your turn," I offered to Stephanie.

Steph shook her head and glanced across the aisle.

Becca sighed, grabbed her carry-on bag, and launched herself from her seat. "Fine, I'll go."

How unprepared I felt at this moment! One of my daughters was excited and raring to go, while the other's emotional state was tender and raw. My husband was on top of the world. And I was on edge, unsure of what to expect or how to be. I ended up choosing the approach most mothers would: to remain strong and positive. All that really mattered was moving forward. I needed to march on.

I watched the Spanish sky brighten outside the window, enjoying my final moments of solitude before the beginning of whatever was about to happen. Meanwhile, the girls and Alan filed into that cramped airplane bathroom one by one, transforming themselves as I had—from sloppy, exhausted messes into dignified representatives of the United States government.

❦

"MR. AMBASSADOR! MRS. SOLOMONT!" THE voice came from the direction of the plane we had just exited. Turning to look back down the jetway, I was puzzled to see Alan's second-in-command, the deputy chief of mission Arnold Chacon, hustling toward us, his smile bright, his blue eyes shining. "Welcome to Madrid! We are so happy to have you here. Please, come this way!" He motioned behind himself, moving us back toward the plane as he explained that he would escort us to a VIP room where Alan would meet some key staff members and the press.

"Lead the way!" Alan said, a bit perplexed but eager. I could tell he was nervous, too, as he cleared his throat, straightened his tie, and followed closely behind Arnold. This was his first time assuming his new ambassadorial stance. He had confided in me his concern about making a good first impression. He wanted to get his first day on the job just right.

Just before we reached the cabin door, Arnold pointed to a set of stairs I hadn't noticed before and said, "This way." The stairs led down to the tarmac, where a van was idling. We all tumbled in.

The van drove as though in circles around the enormous Madrid–Barajas Airport, heading around planes and through tunnels. Ten minutes later, we stopped outside of an unremarkable airport building. "We're here," Arnold announced. "Please follow me, Mr. Ambassador." We climbed out of the van and stepped onto the tarmac.

"What about our luggage?" Becca asked. "And the dog?"

Arnold smiled graciously. "That's all being taken care of. Nothing to worry about." He led us through the entrance and into a large room paneled in a light, yellowish-blond wood where a line of ten professional-looking men and women stood waiting for us. All were impeccably dressed in suits or dresses, despite it being seven thirty on a Saturday morning. This was Alan's formal introduction to his senior team: the head of public affairs, the head of commercial affairs, the defense attaché (director leading all four military branches in an embassy), the head of management, the head of the protocol team, and so on.

We made our way down the line, greeting each person individually. At ambassador school, we had learned the titles of the embassy's major sections, yet I couldn't keep up as everyone rattled off their titles like alphabet soup. How would I ever remember who was who?

I recognized only one person that day: Gary Bagley, the embassy's management counselor. He had already helped answer my questions about what I needed to bring—business cards, stationery, and such. "Oh!" I exclaimed upon shaking his hand, taking in his kind face, silver hair, and genuine smile. "Now I finally know what you look like!"

Alan, on the other hand, was able to identify most everyone in the room. He had meticulously studied each job description and its matching photo before leaving the United States. He stood up straight now and smiled warmly as he went down the line, greeting his senior staff members: "Such a pleasure to meet you." It was quite impressive. I could see the bounce returning to his step as he melted effortlessly into the leadership role he had been called upon to play.

We were invited to sit on a low leather sofa and offered coffee, water, and refreshments. I gasped with excitement as our family dog, Stella Blu—a perfect cream-colored cockapoo (cocker spaniel–poodle mix)—raced across the room, dragging an aide with her. She was all done up for the day as well, having recently visited her hair dresser and sporting a red, white, and blue bandana around her freshly bathed and clipped neck. She gave a rare bark, and licked my and Alan's hands. I was as relieved as she seemed to be; I had worried about how she would fare during the flight. Having heard nightmare stories about pets in the baggage compartment under the plane, I'd always said I would never bring my dog overseas in a crate.

One thing I would learn often during our sojourn in Spain: you should never say never.

The next thing I knew, the doors opened and the press burst in. At least a dozen television reporters, radio talk-show hosts, and photographers formed a semicircle around us. Alan was ready for them. Even though we were still taking Spanish lessons, he had memorized a short statement in Spanish about our arrival. It went something like this: "It's a pleasure to be here. I look forward to strengthening the relationship between our countries. Spain is a very important ally to the United States. We are here to represent President Obama and the people of the United States, and we couldn't be happier to be here."

Talk about showtime! Alan had been just as tired and groggy as the rest of us, but he jumped right into the thick of things. He was incredibly poised and professional, answering questions, smiling, and making eye contact. It was a good thing, too. This was a defining moment, his entry. And Alan knew it.

The press conference continued for about a half hour, a flurry of excited voices and laughter, flashing bulbs, and ringing cellphones. I stood there in my black power dress amid the whirlwind, holding Stella's leash with its distinctive *Boston Globe* dog-waste bag tied on the end of it, responding when someone said something to me, and feeling generally content to be taking it all in. As strange as the scenario was, something felt oddly familiar about it.

I was proud watching Alan work, although my head was also buzzing with a deer-in-the-headlights feeling. *This is my new life*, I kept telling myself, not sure what it all meant. We had barely touched down, and already the country of Spain was saying to us: *Get into character. This is the role you're going to play. We want you "on" all the time.*

This would take some getting used to.

At last, the head of public affairs stood in front of Alan and put his hands up, saying, "Thank you all very much for being here. That's the end of questions for now. We have to get the ambassador and his family home." That's when I realized what was so familiar: it was just like what happens during White House conferences.

Yes, this would take some getting used to. To say the least.

❧

ALTHOUGH OUR PLANE HAD ARRIVED on time that morning, we were setting foot in Spain some three months later than we'd anticipated. All that time, we were in limbo, unsure of how long it would continue or even whether we would ever make it to Spain. First, Alan had to make it through his Senate testimony and confirmation hearing.

One morning back in September, I woke up before dawn to accompany Alan to Washington, DC, for his confirmation hearing. We were driven beneath the State Department and over to the Capitol Building, where a State Department aide escorted us through security and into the hearing room. Alan was quiet and on edge. He had chosen his clothing scrupulously, settling on a red tie with a blue suit and an American flag on his lapel. I wore a black dress and a bright red jacket that I thought would show up well on television. Senate hearings on C-SPAN always showed the first row of people behind the speaker. Today, I was that person behind Alan. That was my job. I was happy to support my husband.

Yet in truth, my job was to sit there and do nothing. *Don't talk to him. Don't ask questions. Don't make jokes. Don't lighten the situation. Nothing. Just let him be.* When you're being vetted for a possible ambassadorship, a hearing is an intense, high-pressure affair. For the spouse, not so much.

Our aide escorted us into one of the Senate chamber rooms, which looked like a typical courtroom: a few tables arranged in a semicircle, from which the senators led the proceedings, facing other tables where the nominee sat. In the back of the room sat the spectators, in five or six rows. I situated myself in the front row as Alan got settled at his table and prepared to testify. At this point, I still thought that as the ambassador's wife, I would be asked to do important things and make a valuable contribution. So I sat there with my mind wandering off into visions of fun, grandeur, and success, smiling and daydreaming about how I would make my mark.

The proceedings did not seem friendly. Although we knew several of the senators personally, we did not walk over to greet them. Protocol dictated who spoke first, who spoke second, who spoke third, and so on. I just smiled and looked on adoringly as Alan read from his seven-minute testimony and then fielded questions for another seven minutes.

One by one, the senators asked their questions about Alan's background and qualifications, and about the basics of America's strategic priorities in Spain. We were both surprised that they were not hardball questions. Still, this was a hurdle we needed to surmount. Alan couldn't get confirmed unless he testified and the committee voted yes. If he screwed up, all the work and preparation he had put in over the past year would be for nothing.

I could hardly believe I was watching my husband's interrogation before the Senate Foreign Relations Committee. Like that first press conference in Spain four months later, it was one of those situations you see on television and in the movies but never imagine yourself being in. As the proceedings continued, I clenched my teeth, clasped my hands tightly, and listened to Alan's carefully chosen words. Every single one mattered, even down to saying *if confirmed* during his responses rather than *when confirmed*.

Yet Alan knew what he was doing. He bobbed and weaved like a pro, comporting himself like his usual brilliant, confident self. I noted how well prepared he was, how smart he sounded, how quick on his feet he thought. Most memorably, he spoke about growing up in Massachusetts, relating how his childhood experience had contributed to his love of politics and his determination to give back. I was very proud to be his wife.

We initially hoped we would hear the good news in about a week, but any hopes we had for a quick confirmation were soon dashed. The senators on the Foreign Relations Committee voted to advance Alan's nomination by the president, so the recommendation went next to the entire Senate for something called "unanimous consent." If one senator doesn't approve or registers any hesitation, the nomination is held up. Nominations can be held up for many different reasons. One senator might require more transportation in his state in exchange for approving a nomination, for example, while another might want a concession on taxation or a foreign policy issue.

After sailing through the committee, Alan hit his first roadblock: Iowa's Senator Chuck Grassley. Alan had served as chairman of the bipartisan board of the Corporation for National and Community Service, which the Clinton administration created in 1993 to house AmeriCorps and other national service programs. Senator Grassley wanted the White House to release papers related to the dismissal of the corporation's inspector general, but the White House refused.

Grassley held the nomination from September through December on that issue alone. The moment he released his hold, Senator Jeff Sessions of Alabama put another hold on for the same reason, and Senator Jim DeMint of South Carolina followed. Those months were extremely difficult for Alan. He wanted that confirmation more than anything.

Throughout the autumn, Alan was consumed with doing anything he could to remove the hold. I, on the other hand, assumed he would eventually be confirmed and took the opportunity to soak up every last bit of home.

Those three months were actually quite fun, and I savored every single day. I had already left my job, so I woke up each morning with a completely open schedule and no agenda. *What would you like to do today?* I asked myself, and then I did it. I took a lot of comfort in this free time.

At the same time, deep-seated anxiety about our future was mounting. I could not begin to imagine living in Spain (or any other country, for that matter). I had been there only once, thirty-five years earlier. What would I do from day to day? I had no idea, and this bothered me. Homesickness was coming on fast—and I hadn't even left home yet.

My fears were made all the worse because I couldn't share them without seeming ungrateful. My friends were so excited for me. No one could relate to my sadness about giving up my everyday life: The greenness of the trees. My daily neighborhood stroll with Stella. Having dinner at our favorite local restaurants. Hiking amid the beauty of New England. The sanctity of our private life. The familiarity of our house and the comforting proximity of our children. The intimacies of friendship.

I made half-hearted appeals for commiseration: "What about apple picking in autumn? What about summer weekends on Cape Cod?" The rebuttal was always the same: "Well, sure, but you'll be in Spain!"

Just after the nomination, on a beautiful Sunday in September, two of my closest friends, Ronni and Alice, threw a goodbye party for me. People blessed me with words of wisdom and sweet goodbyes. We cried. It was beautiful. And three months premature.

Despite the looming uncertainty of Alan's appointment, right after the Jewish High Holidays that same month, we started a three-day process known as the "pack-out," when a moving company packs up the domestic belongings and personal effects that you wish to take to your host country. The movers boxed up over ten thousand pounds of our household possessions, including artwork that needed to be specially crated, cases of American wines we'd hand-selected to serve at embassy events, and of course, our clothing. Everything was on its way to our new home in Madrid.

October 1, November 1, December 1—all came and went, while we remained stateside. As winter approached, we realized that our warm coats had been packed up and shipped ahead. When the freezing weather arrived, I bought myself a new coat, but Alan refused, staging a sort of mini-protest. "We're going to be in Spain. I know it," he insisted, and he went without a winter coat. Instead, trying to keep a sense of humor, he designed T-shirts that showed his face accompanied by the words *Libren Solomont!* We photographed Alan presenting President Obama with one of these "Free Solomont!" shirts.

Finally, on December 23—the same day the US Senate passed health care reform—the senators released the confirmations that were being held up, including Alan's. What a relief! Senator John Kerry, our longtime friend, called with the good news. Alan flew into action, trying to figure out when we could get to Spain. He wanted to leave immediately, but I suggested it would be better for the embassy staff to keep their Christmas vacations intact. So, we settled on the first week in January and began our final preparations.

They say that three things in life are the most stressful: divorce, death, and moving. At Alan's insistence, the main part of our house had been packed up and shipped off long before we had a departure date—so it could have been worse. In the end, we took ten suitcases—all the things we would want for the first few weeks, before our shipment's arrival. And *still* I wondered what I was forgetting. What else did I need? What had I failed to think of? On the day of our flight to Madrid, I walked through our house and took in every room, feeling sad and scared as the same thought ran through my head, over and over: *I can't believe I'm leaving!*

That last day at home was gray, and not just because of the typical cloudy-cold January weather in New England. Even if the sun had been out, I would not have seen it shine. I felt gray *inside*, like a dying tree rooted to the ground. I couldn't move. I just didn't want to leave. That's just the way it was. I was feeling lost and very alone.

I could only hope this gray attitude would fall away quickly in sunny Madrid, as I came face-to-face with my new life.

⚜

AFTER THE PRESS CONFERENCE IN a Madrid–Barajas Airport VIP room, Alan and I were escorted to a long black Cadillac with United States and Department of State flags flanking its windshield. Two men on either side of the limousine simultaneously opened its rear doors. Somehow, I remembered to walk around and slide in from the driver's side, just as I had learned in ambassador school.

For security reasons, the spouse always—without exception—sits in the rear driver's-side seat. That way, the ambassador can sit on the curbside, behind the front passenger. If a threat ever arises, the security guard who occupies the front passenger seat can get the ambassador out to safety quickly and easily.

In the ambassador seminar, one of the spouses raised her hand and asked, "Excuse me, but what about me?"

The response: "We'll do the best we can, ma'am."

As we drove through Madrid toward the US embassy and the attached diplomatic residence, I still couldn't believe it was happening: Here I was, driving through a European capital city in a motorcade— our very own motorcade. It felt surreal. Police motorcycles with flashing blue lights led the way, and behind us followed a van carrying Becca and Stephanie, finished off by another set of motorcycles. The vehicle's doors were heavy—armored, we were told—and the windows were thicker and smaller than normal car windows. When I looked outside, it was difficult to see much of anything.

A text message came through from Stephanie: *Doesn't the ambassador stop for red lights?*

No, apparently he doesn't. I hadn't even noticed. For some reason, I had assumed that on our first time seeing Madrid, we would lumber through the city. Didn't motorcades usually travel at a relatively slow pace? But our car just *flew*, blasting through the streets of Madrid— which, at eight thirty on a Saturday morning, were empty.

Madrid is not exactly a morning town.

Squinting through the window, I could just make out apartment buildings, grand boulevards, and serene city streets. No skyscrapers, just small buildings. Although I caught only glimpses and flashes of this attractive city—the day was as dreary and gray as the one I'd left behind in America—my heart flickered with excitement.

Fifteen minutes passed. Then our car turned and climbed a small hill. I peered out just in time to see uniformed Spanish police officers saluting the car, and one half of a humungous steel gate slowly opening onto our new residence.

Alan and I had been on a virtual tour of the house, narrated by Cristina Álvarez, the residence manager, in her cute Spanish accent: "Mr. Ambassador and Madam, we welcome you to your home in Madrid, Spain! I am going to show you through the residence so you can see the beautiful house you are going to be living in!" I had thought the video prepared us. After all, Cristina had walked us through every room of the house. But now, as the car pulled through the gate, I could only shake my head in disbelief.

No photo, no video, no virtual tour could have done this place justice. It was a large, two-story modernist house made of concrete, situated on a hill entirely enclosed by tall fences. A rolling lawn stretched out in front, and the driveway cut through the lawn's center. The front steps were lovely and grand. They made quite a statement.

We came to a stop and stepped out of the car to find the entire residence staff assembled on the steps to greet us: Cristina, our residence manager; Antonio, the butler; two footmen named Carlos and Bryon; Adelina, the head maid; two additional maids, Ani and Noemi; Gustavo, the chef; Rosita, or "Rosi," the cook. All in uniform, all standing proudly with big smiles to welcome us. It was very *Downton Abbey*.

Alan and I made our way up the steps, greeting each staff member on the way up. "*Señor Embajador y Señora*" was the response each time. Only Cristina, our virtual tour guide, spoke English.

It was hard to connect with the staff in that moment. Strict protocol shaped their interactions with us, reflecting a strong sense of social hierarchy. I just wanted them to like me. Little did I know, they were *programmed* to like me—just there to please, to make our lives better and easier. That was their job. As I would come to find out, they did it well.

Once we reached the top of the steps, with our daughters trailing behind, Cristina took us on the live-action version of the tour while the rest of the staff went back to work. The footmen carried our luggage inside. All of it, even my purse.

Through the entryway and a little bit further, we found ourselves in a grand foyer. "This is where you'll have your receiving lines," Cristina said, and guided us all around the ground-floor level. On this main floor were a formal living room, a formal dining room, a piano room, and a few other rooms for entertaining guests, including bedrooms for visitors. The entire "representational floor"—where we would hold public or representational events—was decorated in antiques and antique-style furnishings dominated by dark mahogany. In the dining room, a mahogany dining table with a huge breakfront, and mahogany sideboards. In the living room, mahogany end tables. It all evoked great importance and luxury. I was grateful for the virtual tour, but the real thing was much more glamorous than I had anticipated.

Cristina led us up a bridal staircase. "Sir, Madam, these are your private quarters," she explained. "This is where the family lives. No one comes up here, other than the staff. This is all just for you."

A former ambassador had renovated the private floor at his own expense, fashioning a supremely beautiful place to live, and we were lucky to be the beneficiaries of his discerning taste. The private quarters were like a magnificent New York City apartment, nicely furnished throughout, with a living room that felt much more family-oriented than the one downstairs; a plush sofa and two overstuffed chairs facing a television; and built-in, floor-to-ceiling bookcases. Like the rest of the apartment, the bookcases were completely bare—waiting for our personal touch.

The bedroom attached to our living room was colored in soft greens and peaches, and featured a king-sized bed with a gorgeous upholstered headboard. We also had private, his-and-hers bathrooms, and—I will confess—the nicest closet ever. This thing was *huge*, with yards of space to hang clothing. In the middle was one of those built-in pieces with his-and-hers drawers on both sides and a green suede surface ideal for folding or packing clothing.

Down a corridor from our private rooms were three bedrooms, all en suite, intended for our personal guests. And down another corridor was an additional living room along with a dining room and a kitchen, which we would use for our private meals.

We were impressed.

Following Cristina into the kitchen, I found myself feeling good about the apartment overall. Maybe this place would come to feel like a home to me. We could be comfortable here. I mean, we had everything we needed, right? A bed, some couches, a roof over our heads, a bit of privacy.

On the other hand, I was also feeling impatient. Would this ever really feel like home? My uncomfortable, overtired, jet-lagged self just wanted to feel settled in. I could sense that Alan felt antsy as well, though for entirely different reasons. He was itching to get to work, and not really worried much about his living space. He took quick glances and moved faster through each room than I did.

Passing through that kitchen, we realized we were starving. The staff sprang into action, bringing gigantic chocolate chip muffins that were moist, tasty, exquisite—and the size of three ordinary muffins. I couldn't have eaten a whole one even if I had wanted to, although the girls certainly tried. The chef also made us delicious eggs, and I learned my first Spanish meal phrase: *huevos revueltos*. Scrambled eggs on fine china, with gold rim and the Department of State seal. Unbelievable.

From there, we scattered to our rooms to unpack. The staff fought to unpack for us, but on this I would not budge. The truth was, I desperately needed a nap.

※

I AWOKE ABOUT FIVE HOURS later to the afternoon light streaming into the room of light greens and peaches. Alan was puttering about, pulling ties and toiletries from his suitcases.

Alan's first task as ambassador was presenting a copy of his official papers, indicating that he was President Obama's representative, to Spain's foreign minister, Miguel Ángel Moratinos. Spain had been without a US ambassador for the past year, and the Spanish government eagerly awaited Alan's arrival. "So?" he asked, walking through the bathroom door and holding out his arms. "Will this do?"

From the bed, I smiled at him, handsome in a dark gray suit. "Looks great."

He kissed me on the cheek, and I asked when exactly he'd be back. "Probably be a few hours," he replied.

As the door closed behind him, I settled upright into a stack of fluffy pillows. Outside the window, Madrid looked dreary—a few snowflakes drifted in the wind, mingling with the constant rain that rustled the leaves of the trees. Despite the weather, I itched to get out of the house and explore until I felt more comfortable in my surroundings. I changed my clothes and went to ask Becca and Steph to join me.

I found them both sound asleep. "Come on, you two! Let's get up and go out!"

"Ugh, Mom!" Becca growled, head under her pillow.

Steph yawned, pulling her comforter over her eyes. "Leave us alone! More . . . sleep . . ."

I tugged on their exposed feet, then shook their legs and arms. "Don't you want to explore the city? Let's walk Stella!"

"Sure," Becca agreed. "In, like, five minutes."

"Ten!" Steph said, sticking her hand in the air. "Ten more minutes."

"No, no more minutes," I insisted. "Let's go!"

"*Ugh!*" they moaned in unison, throwing back the sheets and climbing out of bed. They pulled on clothes and, a few minutes later, met me in the hall.

"But, Mom, how will we get back in?" Stephanie asked.

Oh. Right.

Nobody had given me a key to the house. I didn't even know how to call downstairs to ask Cristina what to do.

Luckily, in houses like this, things just magically *happen*. By the time the girls and I reached the bottom of the stairs, Carlos the footman had appeared. With Stella. On her leash. With the *Boston Globe* bag tied to the end of it.

I hadn't said a word about wanting to go out, so how did the staff know? Had they overheard us? Were there little cameras everywhere? No. Somehow, they just knew. They were that good.

"Oh! Hello!" I said, waving and taking Stella's leash. "We're going out. How do I get back into the house?"

Carlos cocked his head to the side and looked at me inquisitively. Of course: no English. I had forgotten.

"Um, a key?" I motioned, walking over to the grand, wooden front door. Thank goodness for universal sign language.

Carlos smiled and nodded his head. "*Sí, sí, Señora. No se preocupe.*" (Don't worry.) He opened the door to let us out and pointed to a small doorbell to the right of its frame.

"Of course, right. Thank you!"

The girls laughed, and once again it struck me how different my life had suddenly become. With a fully staffed house and security guards at the gates, what use was a key?

We walked down the long, cobblestone driveway to the gates, where a security guard opened a door to let us out. And then we were on the streets of Madrid.

Gazing up at the grand architecture all around us, we decided to look for the Serrano—Madrid's premier shopping street, like Newbury Street in Boston or Madison Avenue in New York City—but we lacked any clue to where we were going. Our quest led us up a street called the Castellana, a beautiful, broad, busy boulevard lined with huge trees, which proved to be a nice distraction. We meandered its spacious sidewalks, passing ornate *palacitas*, or "little palaces." Some had fences around them; others had gardens. We began to pass taller buildings, stacked with offices, and looked for the Serrano as cars whipped by us.

Our family likes to joke about my excellent sense of direction—my "built-in GPS," they call it. But on that day, with everything going on, I simply could *not* find the Serrano. I hadn't brought a map, because this was supposed to be my home. I lived here. No maps needed. Nor were there signs, but I could've sworn that the Castellana and the Serrano intersected (little did I know they are *parallel* streets). I had this fierce need to figure it all out on my own, on day one. I didn't need any help.

To make matters worse, we were bewildered by the traffic patterns, which didn't work the same way they do in the States. In the States, the cars stop at a traffic light, before the intersection. In Madrid, sometimes the cars go *into* the intersection, and pedestrians just have to figure it out.

The Castellana is wider than most American highways, with three lanes of traffic moving in each direction and an island in the middle. It is definitely wider than the Massachusetts Turnpike, which I was used to. As pedestrians, we had to somehow cross this street.

We traversed the first section, stopping in the middle, and then crossed the other three lanes. To make it through the westbound lanes, we had to cross again, never with green going all the way. At each place we stopped, the traffic light was a different color. Meanwhile, cars flew past us at top speed. Trust me, it was extremely stressful.

Nevertheless, we walked on through the streets of Madrid, heading in one direction for a while and then turning back and retracing our steps. Frustrated with myself, and depressed that I couldn't find the damn Serrano, I finally decided to surrender. I had wanted this little sightseeing adventure to inspire the girls with excitement about Spain—especially Becca, who had never quite warmed up to the idea—but I couldn't even organize our first shopping trip.

Trudging back toward our residence, we came across a building that was breathtaking, with layers of arched windows and beautiful Spanish mosaic tiles from sidewalk to roof: the ABC (pronounced "Ah Bay Say"). Wandering inside, we discovered that this building was a cross between a traditional American shopping mall and an office building, with shops located on a seemingly endless number of floors, all connected by a winding ramp. The girls grinned as they craned their heads, taking it in. They were insistent: they needed a hair dryer that ran on 220 volts. We would get our shopping done after all.

Or maybe not.

A security guard approached us, pointing at Stella with his brow furrowed. "*No perros! Usted no debe tener el perro. No perros.*"

What was he saying? I had no clue.

Both Becca and Steph had taken Spanish in school. "Mom, pick Stella up," Steph urged. "She can only be in here if you hold her." She apologized to the guard ("*Lo siento!*") as I hastily collected Stella.

Even though she is a relatively small dog, Stella got heavy after a while. We found a hair dryer that we liked and, with that small victory under my belt, walked back to the residence—a trip that took only five minutes.

The instant we rounded the corner, the security guard opened the gate. We made our way up the driveway, and as soon as we approached the foot of the steps, Carlos opened the front door. Everything was so programmed: when they saw us coming down the street, they knew. They got ready. When security opened the gate, someone rang the house, and the footman came to open the door and welcome us back.

Magic.

Back in the relative comfort of my bedroom, I reflected on my first outing in Spain. In truth, I was overwhelmed. No matter how badly I wanted to feel at home, nothing was the way I was used to. Women were dressed in heels and *furs* while fulfilling daily errands. Stella wasn't allowed to walk through stores. I couldn't find the main street. And I didn't even have a key to my home. I had no control, and I wasn't used to that.

Similar feelings would stay with me for the first few months in Spain: disorientation, uncertainty, sadness. I handled them as best I could. One Sunday morning, Alan and I were lying in bed reading the newspapers and listening to music—Alan had bought me a stereo system as a gift. A song by the artist Brett Dennen came on, called "Darlin', Do Not Fear." I quietly sang along to the lyrics:

> *When I arrived in my old set of clothes,*
> *I was half a world away from my home . . .*
> *Darlin', do not fear what you don't really know.*

The thought of that song still transports me, every time, back to my bed in Madrid on that cold January day. I wept silently, but Alan still noticed. He was loving his work, loving his role as ambassador, loving every new experience. In the face of such enthusiasm, it was hard for me to share my difficulties adjusting.

Then Alan hugged me, and just being held by him made me feel better. I didn't say much. I didn't need to—he got it.

❦

TO CELEBRATE OUR FIRST NIGHT in Spain, Arnold and the senior embassy team arranged a dinner at a steakhouse in central Madrid, near the Royal Palace. This time Alan, the girls, and I were driven over in a van with normal windows, operated at a leisurely pace and obeying all traffic laws, so I was able to get a good look at the city. It struck me as beautiful, especially at night. The nineteenth-century stone buildings were lit up, twinkling amid the falling snowflakes. Big, urban squares pulsated with nightlife. Majestic fountains, glittering and gushing, popped up on nearly every street. The architecture had personality and old-world charm, with rooftops populated by statues of Roman and Greek gods. It was all so different from the United States—almost too picturesque to be real.

The van stopped and Alan's security guards escorted us into the restaurant's back room. It was dimly lit with a massive, square, wooden table in the center of the room, all set and ready for guests. Some members of Alan's team who had greeted us at the airport were there with their spouses, and they all reintroduced themselves. Everyone was incredibly kind.

"How are you tonight?" they asked.

"How old are your kids?"

"Where in Boston do you live?"

We reciprocated: "How long have you lived in Madrid? Where else have you been posted?" These were casual, surface-level conversations, but polite and well-meaning nonetheless.

I can't say I felt comfortable at dinner. I was too busy being "on." I couldn't very well sit down at the table and announce, *I'm exhausted!*

And homesick! And your intersections are weird! I'm not going to talk to anyone. I knew that I had to be friendly and sociable. And I *was* friendly and sociable. I really did want to make a good first impression—and of course, I knew that everybody wanted me to like them as well.

Alan, meanwhile, was *glowing*. At one point early in the evening, he stood and raised his glass. "What I've learned is that one of the things ambassadors do is give toasts. So allow me to offer a toast on behalf of Susan, Becca, and Stephanie, and how wonderful it is for us all to be here together."

"Hear, hear!" his team members called back.

Arnold stood up then, offering a toast of his own. "Welcome, Mr. Ambassador. We welcome you here. We very much look forward to working with you!"

"Hear, hear!" came the response again.

And then the red wine just *flowed*. There was enough to go around the table ten times over—which, as I would learn, is just so typical of the Spanish people.

Although we were at an Argentinian steakhouse (an unusual place to go on your first night in Spain), the staff did introduce us to a wonderful Spanish dish called *pimientos del padres*—small, fried peppers that are kind of sweet. We also ordered *tortilla española*, a traditional potato and egg dish that resembles a quiche, and *jamón ibérico* (Iberian ham), a beloved Spanish staple. You just pick it up and eat it with your fingers, like French fries—except it's cured ham.

When dinner concluded, we strolled over to one of Europe's largest palaces: the Palacio Real de Madrid, or Royal Palace of Madrid—not the king's official residence, but rather where state banquets and ceremonies take place. There's one grand boulevard leading up to the Palacio, ending in a pedestrian-only walk patrolled by security. By this time, it was eleven thirty at night, and the Royal Palace was shining bright so as to show its enormous outline against the sky. Standing there, I saw little else—just palace and sky. Turning away from the Palacio offered a glimpse of the Plaza de Oriente, an open square that's more of a garden with huge statues of Spanish kings on horses, their swords raised high. I was surrounded by true Spanish regality.

"It's too cold! Let's head back to the car!" someone suggested.

"Sure thing," Alan replied.

As if by magic, once again, our van was already lumbering up the pathway for us—the pedestrian-only pathway, where no cars are allowed. Well, none except ours, apparently.

Standing next to the Palacio that night, I had a special moment—an epiphany of sorts. I let out a breath and thought, *I'm going to like it here.*

I had moved to Europe, to a world-class city that was beautiful, almost a fairy tale with its palaces and royal family. I was going to get to know it. I was going to learn its streets. I was not going to get lost every day while trying to find the Serrano. I was going to understand this place and its people. I was going to build a life for myself and find a way to contribute.

At this realization, a fog lifted off me, and a voice deep inside said, "This is going to be exciting." And I believed it.

TWO

FROM SEA
TO SHINING SEA

ORE THAN A HALF-CENTURY AGO, on March 8, 1960, a small US Navy plane en route to the US military base in Rota, Spain, was cruising over the Sierra Nevada mountain range when it passed through a violent blizzard. Bobbing and thrashing through the fog and against the whipping winds, the plane dipped too low, and its right wing slammed into a remote, snowy peak. Seconds later, the *Ciudad de Madrid*, named after Spain's capital city, crash-landed at the edge of a gorge, mere feet away from what would have been a devastating drop.

Although all twenty-four passengers on board survived the impact, most were injured and unable to walk. With temperatures at the site well below freezing, the two navy pilots made the difficult decision to leave the plane to seek help. After a painful six-hour hike, they came across the small shepherding town of Jérez del Marquesado, in the region of Andalucía. The pilots approached a townsperson and tried to speak to him, but he ran away, thinking that Martians were invading the area. At that time, no one in the town had a television or had ever seen a plane. No one had even heard anyone speak any language other than Spanish.

The pilots pushed on, reaching the local post of the Guardia Civil, the national police. Unable to speak Spanish, they communicated what had happened using a paper airplane made out of a newspaper. Once the guards understood that the crewmen were injured and in danger of freezing to death, they sounded alarm bells throughout the town. Before long, a string of men and boys as young as fifteen formed a rescue party and set off up the mountain, tunneling through waist-deep snow, dragging cloth stretchers and supplies for the stranded navy men. As Jérez del Marquesado was a poor town, most rescuers were ill-prepared for such a mission—no warm clothes, no boots, no flashlights—yet they took off on foot, compelled by their duty to aid others whose lives were at risk.[1]

After two days of working around the clock, carrying the men across treacherous terrain without ambulances, the rescuers managed to move all the Americans down the mountain. Some townspeople stayed overnight in the plane with the survivors to ensure their safety.

"It was worth it," said Antonio Lorente, who also spent the night in the plane, awaiting assistance. "We did not know what happened, but only that it was necessary to help human beings." All twenty-four naval passengers survived the ordeal, a feat that many attribute to the quick help rendered by the local inhabitants. A rescue at 7,600 feet above sea level on the edge of a cliff was not merely heroic—it was record-setting in the annals of aviation.[2]

Soon afterward, US ambassador John Davis Lodge visited the town to personally thank the people of Jérez del Marquesado. He received a

---

1   Jose Valentin, "Villagers Help Crashed Martians," *EuroWeekly*, March 1, 2013, https://archive.euroweeklynews.com/columnists/113373-villagers-help-crashed-martians.

2   Ben Tisdale, "Spanish Village, Remembers 50th Anniversary of 'Skymaster' Rescue," *Navy*, September 11, 2010, https://www.navy.mil/submit/display.asp?story_id=55824.

very warm and celebratory welcome. The entire town filled the streets to catch a wave or smile from Lodge. He announced that the US Navy would donate the remains of the plane to Jérez del Marquesado, and during that year's thaw, parts were collected piece by piece. Proud townspeople put electrical panels, fuse hatches, and pieces of scrap metal on display at their homes for all to see, and some pieces are still displayed on those balconies today. The townspeople sold the bulk of the plane's scrap metal, using the proceeds to develop the town's first running water system.

This event represents a pivotal moment in the history of Jérez del Marquesado. Fifty years later, in September 2010, town officials commemorated the event with a joyful celebration uniting survivors, rescuers, and the US ambassador at that time—Alan Solomont.

Alan and I flew into the nearby town of Granada, which is home to the Alhambra, an enormous eighth-century fortress built by the Moors who occupied that region. We were eight months into our tenure, and this historic site was high on my list of places to visit, but we didn't have time to visit the famous site itself. Instead, we enjoyed a light breakfast, including fresh-squeezed orange juice from local fruit, with the mayor of Granada at a restaurant overlooking the Alhambra.

The weather was a gorgeous eighty degrees, and the sky, a clear, deep blue. As we climbed the winding mountain roads toward Jérez del Marquesado in an oversized, armored SUV, I struggled to glimpse the views through tiny, bulletproof windows. The southwestern region of Spain doesn't get much rain in the spring or summer, so the rocky landscape was brown and arid, speckled with pine trees. After an hour of climbing, we finally reached the village entrance. The vehicle was too large to fit through the cobblestone streets, so we stopped at the edge of the town.

When our driver, Alejandro, came around to open the doors, I saw that the entire town had congregated and was waiting to greet us. Everyone was smiling and cheering and waving, like in those giant victory parades you see on television. Men and women hung from balconies and out of windows with children perched on their shoulders. People cheered, "Long live the United States! Welcome, the Ambassador! Welcome, Mrs. Ambassador!"

Alan rounded the car to stand next to me as the town's mayor and formal delegation made their way over. The mayor kissed me on both cheeks and handed me a huge bouquet of flowers. He firmly shook Alan's hand before motioning for us to follow him toward the town square.

The streets were a sea of people pulsating around us. I caught Alan's eye, and my smile widened slightly as we shared the secret joy of this experience we would never forget. *Can you believe this?* my expression said. *How amazing!*

And it was so unexpected. Anytime we traveled, Alan would receive documents briefing him on what we would encounter. He would learn about the history of a place, the people we would be meeting, the nature of the official business, and so on. Though we had thoroughly read the briefing, we did not have *this* in mind. I'd expected maybe a small ceremony in the mayor's office, or a dedication at some site related to the amazing rescue. I had no idea we would be helping preside over such a momentous celebration.

How much pride this tiny town took in its act of heroism! Alan and I shook hands and waved our way through the crowd, finally making it to the town center accompanied by throngs of followers. Underneath the town hall's arched entrance was a grand platform with a podium facing rows of benches and chairs. We sat down and were treated to performances of local music and dance. Then came the real surprise: naval officers had located some of the survivors months prior to the ceremony, and the town had identified some of the men who had trekked into the hills to rescue the wounded. These men stood up and received public recognition. The clapping went on for long stretches of time.

They had aged significantly, of course, and most were not in the best of health. The Americans had brought their families, all there to express their gratitude. "The highlight of attending this trip was to see the survivors interact with their rescuers," one naval officer recalled. "It was emotional, and you could feel the mutual respect, understanding, and admiration. The townspeople of Jérez del Marquesado enveloped the survivors with hospitality beyond their wildest imaginations."[3]

I couldn't have said it better myself.

The statements of the rescuers, such as, "Fifty years ago, this small town did what anyone should do . . ." sounded overly modest to me. How many people among us would hike ten kilometers into the woods during a raging blizzard to rescue complete strangers? That's not ordinary heroism. That's something else entirely.

Each rescuer and crash survivor received a beautiful Andalusian ceramic plate, about eighteen inches in diameter, with an image of the town and the mountains behind it. At the ceremony's conclusion, Alan mounted the podium and received a ceramic plate of his own, which today hangs proudly on our wall in Weston. He delivered an emotional speech commemorating what Jérez del Marquesado did for our country. Then Alan and I shook hands with each man.

Afterward, a large group of us went to a local restaurant for a light lunch of *jamón* and *queso* (cheese), little sandwiches called *bocadillos*, and beer and wine. Everybody wanted to pose with Alan and me for a photograph, and they thanked us again and again for coming.

To my mind, it should have flowed in the opposite direction, with us Americans taking the lead in expressing our thanks to the people of this rural village. *How wonderful it must be*, I thought, *to live in a place where generosity is the natural instinct.*

---

3 Tisdale, "Spanish Village, Remembers."

And how much the people of Jérez del Marquesado had to teach us about life!

※

BACK AT AMBASSADOR SCHOOL, THE State Department instructors had emphasized the need for ambassadors to maintain a presence throughout the countries to which they were assigned. "Remember," they told us, "you're not the ambassador to Madrid. You're the ambassador to *Spain*, so you'll need to get out of Madrid often." They didn't have to ask me twice.

When I imagined what life might be like as a diplomatic spouse, one of the most attractive elements was the travel involved. Before crossing the Atlantic, I researched dozens of places in Spain that appealed to me. I knew what I wanted to see, where I wanted to eat, and where I wanted to stay. A picture had formed in my mind of Alan and me enjoying these travels together. We would tour the many historic and cultural sites of Spain, making memories that we'd share the rest of our lives. We would spend days sunning on sparkling Mediterranean beaches . . . wandering the streets of Spanish cities . . . eating romantic dinners at fabulous restaurants . . . soaking up local culture at neighborhood cafés . . . and touring out-of-the-way villages and rural areas . . .

Hard work notwithstanding, all this and more came to pass; and for that, I will be forever grateful. I had many, many unforgettable experiences, and I enjoyed the privilege of getting to know the wonderful people of Spain as well as our own military personnel stationed in the country. Yet travel in Spain, like most aspects of my life there, also required some growth on my part—as well as a considerable adjustment of my expectations.

The growth began early on, during a three-day trip to Barcelona in February 2010 when I made my first important touristic discovery: high-speed rail. Barcelona is a seven-hour drive from Madrid but, as we soon learned, only about three hours on the high-speed train. Compared with any US train service, including Amtrak's Acela Express (the country's fastest rail service), travel on Spain's AVE was spectacular. The train left and arrived on time. You had to go through security, but you didn't have to arrive an hour early. The train was clean, smooth, and quiet. Onboard movies and decent food enticed passengers. High-speed rail is far and away the easiest, most comfortable way to get around in Spain.

Upon our arrival, Alan was whisked away to meet with Barcelona's political leaders, including the mayor (*el alcade*) and the equivalent of the region's governor (*el presidente*). Much of his day was packed with meeting after meeting. Lucky for me, we were traveling with Joan and Steve, two of our very best friends from home. The three of us set off with a protocol officer to view the city's spectacular tourist sites and dazzling municipal buildings. For me, the highlight was visiting the sites of Spain's most famous and visionary architect, Antoni Gaudí. His masterpiece is a church, the Sagrada Familia, which he began in 1882; he died before finishing, however, and it remains incomplete to this day. Although Gaudí's drawings were destroyed in a fire, the models he used still exist, and skilled hands faithfully continue the work with an eye toward completion by 2030.

We toured the Sagrada Familia with Jordi Bonet i Armengol, lead architect of the construction and renovation project—a man who has spent nearly three decades working to complete the church. Jordi's father assisted Gaudí during his lifetime. Introduced to the project in the 1930s, at age seven, Jordi was just as passionate, driven, and dedicated to the mission as ever. Talk about a labor of love!

Jordi led us through a construction site, maneuvering around scaffolding, workmen elevators, and—from 170 meters (560 feet) up—views that made my stomach drop. As we learned, a new phase of the church would be completed later that year, and Pope Benedict XVI had already announced he would attend the opening. Now, that's some pressure to get the job done.

This church and some of the surrounding monuments Gaudí created were spectacular—playful, creative, and unique, the product of genius. And although I felt grateful for the intimate encounter with such magnificent architecture, I was also aware of the disparity between my experience and my husband's. Alan was off to sit in the power seat among prominent people, chatting about important issues, and there I was, experiencing Spain as a tourist.

This disparity was, of course, as it should be. Alan was the ambassador representing the United States on official business. He and his staff had put a lot of thought into exactly whom he should meet and what they should discuss. I didn't hold an official position. I was just the spouse. Yet I wanted to be busy too.

Part of it was ego. I was used to attending important meetings and forming useful relationships with people. But part of it *wasn't* a matter of ego at all. I wanted to contribute to society in a meaningful way.

That day in Barcelona, I wondered if I would ever find my groove in Spain. Alan had slipped into his so naturally. Even though we had been in the country for only a month, he was out having business meals, meeting with regional government leaders, taking high-level calls, working on important military issues, sitting for interviews with every major newspaper, appearing on television programs—and generally enjoying great happiness and fulfillment. His fountain was overflowing with invitations and opportunities. In comparison, my fountain was, well, a bit dry.

That I couldn't enjoy travel as I had hoped, during our official visits at least, was something I would have to accept. And by and large, I did accept it, and came to enjoy being a professional tourist. Yet I never quite got used to having no concrete purpose while visiting all the regions of Spain.

Given the 24/7 nature of Alan's work, his ambassadorship was omnipresent, wedging its way between us. And I couldn't help my wishful thinking. If I wasn't going to be working, I wanted to share my time with my husband. My idea of fun wasn't going off to an exotic city and experiencing it by myself.

Alan did make a special effort to include me whenever he could, which made for many memorable experiences. That first afternoon in Barcelona, he conducted a forum at a local university before a packed auditorium of aspiring journalists. He gave a fifteen-minute speech on US–Spain relations, and then allowed the students to interview him as if they were conducting a real broadcast press conference. Just like at his hearing at the Senate Foreign Relations Committee, Alan was simply wonderful: intelligent, funny, quick on his feet. He had students stand up when they posed questions, and he fired a few back, establishing a lively and entertaining rapport. I watched from the front row, delighting in the spectacle. I especially appreciated it when Alan said, "You know, everybody, I'm here in Spain with my wife. Feel free to ask her questions as well." They didn't, but his gesture meant a lot, and he repeated it at many of his public appearances.

In the city of Sevilla, where Alan met with the American equivalent of a chamber of commerce, he insisted that I take a seat at the table. The conversation touched on several economic challenges facing the Andalusian business community, including Spanish olive oil manufacturers. Spain produces more olives than any other country in the world, and Spanish olives are arguably the globe's best. We learned that many other countries use Spanish olives to make their olive oil, but the packaging reads *Italian olive oil* or *Greek olive oil*. As a result, consumers are misled, and Spanish olive oil goes underappreciated.

As the growers expressed their frustrations with the economy, I had a chance to put my own business insights to work and talk about marketing and brand exposure. When people think of Spain, they imagine fiestas, flamenco, and bullfighting. They think of an "easy does it" work ethic, complete with two-hour siestas in the afternoon. But that's not what the country is all about. Spain is a modern, advanced society, and for the past thirty-five years, it has grown into a dynamic democracy as well. The country boasts talented, globally competitive companies like the retail giant Inditex, best known for its worldwide Zara brand; Iberdrola, a global energy company that operates wind farms across the United States; and Ferrovial, a multinational construction company that builds airports, toll roads, and other large infrastructure projects. In Spain, people work hard to produce high-quality goods—and these olive farmers were a case in point.

I was cautious in my comments, trying to strike a positive note and offering constructive criticism only sparingly. But Spanish products and the country's overall image needed an effective branding consultant to help spread the word about the country's true worth and how valuable their products are. Spain did in fact establish Marca España, a government initiative to "brand" and promote Spanish products and tourism, and the country itself. The Spanish government likewise convened a panel of experts to help promote the Spanish brand in everything from racecar driving and manufacturing to food and holidays. I won't claim credit for these developments, although that afternoon in Sevilla, I did feel that I could contribute something substantive to the conversation.

The insight that most bolstered my confidence that day belonged to Juan Rivera, the husband of Maritheresa Frain, the consular officer for the Andalucía region. Rivera is a noted business professor affiliated with universities across Spain and the United States. As he listened to the conversation with the Andalusian business leaders and olive industry representatives, it occurred to him to have me speak at other meetings of students and business leaders. About a year later, Alan and I received another invitation to visit Sevilla, and this time I was the invited guest. I addressed an audience of Spanish businesswomen and female entrepreneurs, including the female founder of Telepizza, a pizza delivery service that became like the Domino's of Spain.

I enjoyed doing official appearances on my own, and I began receiving invitations to speak at a variety of events. I keynoted a conference on fundraising and philanthropy, which are not really part of the culture in Spain. Since philanthropy is my business, I was able to share best practices in fundraising, including basic principles and tactics. On another occasion, I met with leaders of Spanish and American companies to discuss issues relating to women: How do you *really* promote women to senior positions? What's the glass ceiling all about? What will it take to shatter it?

In these events and others, I caught a glimmer of my own professional self. It was nice to feel needed and wanted again—to contribute to our diplomatic mission, to do something important. I didn't want my travels in Spain to become purely an opportunity for leisure and diversion. I wanted them to mean something.

※

EVEN WHEN I WASN'T CONTRIBUTING professionally during our travels, I found personal joy and enrichment in other ways. One of these was my ongoing education in military affairs and the experiences of American servicepeople abroad. The US ambassador oversees all branches of the military stationed in the country, except for soldiers under combat command. In this capacity, Alan and I had a chance to visit important US military facilities in Spain and to learn about the lives of those in uniform.

In April 2012, I joined Alan on a visit to the naval base in Rota. A Spanish vice admiral commands Rota Naval Base with shared use by the US military. We flew to Cádiz, a beautiful old city located in the southwest corner of Spain, near the meeting point of the Mediterranean Sea and the Atlantic Ocean. Cádiz is said to be Europe's oldest city, founded by Phoenicians around 1100 BC. It's also near the seaport of Palos de la Frontera, from which Columbus set sail, and which is the birthplace of Spain's first constitution, known as *La Pepa*. This colorful name reflects the day of the constitution's adoption, St. Joseph's Day on March 19, 1812. In Spain, Pepe is a nickname for Joseph. Interestingly, the constitution is gendered female—*La Pepa*.

From the city, we drove an hour along small highways to the military base's entrance. I had never seen a military base before and was surprised at the size of this one. It was a city in and of itself, with a port, a small airport, schools, a hospital, recreation facilities, a hotel, and (my personal favorite) a Navy Exchange, or NEX. The NEX is a commissary for military personnel and their families, a place where they can buy American products for their personal use. Going to the NEX at Rota was like going to a giant Target or CVS. After checking in to the hotel, Alan and I wound up buying a pair of sneakers, some cosmetics, and some *Modern Family* DVDs. To me, so far from home, these were extraordinary finds.

Later that night, the base commander hosted a reception for us, inviting enlisted soldiers and officers alike. I learned that the US Navy uses Rota when deploying its ships to the Mediterranean, the Middle East, northern Africa, and elsewhere. I was particularly interested to learn about the Fast Action Troop Unit based in Rota, a unit of Marines that can deploy quickly to protect US diplomatic facilities in the region.

My education continued when Secretary of the Navy Ray Mabus came to Spain and invited us to accompany him to the port of Cartagena, on the Mediterranean coast. We flew from Madrid on the secretary's plane. A sweet, down-to-earth man, Secretary Mabus (even though he insisted upon being called Ray, not "Mr. Secretary") related that serving in this naval post was the most amazing job he'd ever had. One of his goals was to make the entire US Navy fleet more environmentally friendly—by reducing its reliance on fossil fuels by 50 percent and by increasing the use of renewable energy such as solar and wind power. Our conversation was truly riveting.

Once in Cartagena, we toured our country's newest aircraft carrier in the region, the USS *George H. W. Bush*. If you have not spent time on an aircraft carrier, you cannot imagine how enormous these ships are. Weighing over ninety thousand tons, the ship has a flight deck capable of accommodating seventy-five planes and helicopters, and it carries a crew of five thousand. A very special part of this trip was meeting Rear Admiral Nora Tyson, the first woman to command an aircraft carrier strike group (which includes an aircraft carrier plus several other naval vessels). From Secretary Mabus, I learned that Tyson's promotion had blazed a path for many other servicewomen.

While small in stature, Tyson had a powerful presence. She had the poise and authority to command a five-thousand-person crew, but she was also personable and warm, able to connect to others in conversation. Admiral Tyson showed us around the ship, including the flight deck. The wind just *whipped* across that deck, and I was relieved that Secretary Mabus's team had advised me not to wear a dress or heels—this was no place for high fashion.

We climbed up ladders and walked across the deck, watching planes take off and land. These jets go from zero to 150 miles per hour in less than three seconds, and they slow down at the same pace upon landing. Amazing!

Also impressive was the precision of the flight operations. On the flight deck, markings indicated exactly where each and every plane belonged. The deck was spotless, and the sailors all wore different colored helmets and uniforms representing their unique roles. In the control room, the crew had assembled an operations board laid out with little color-coded squares. You know the hotels and houses you buy in the game Monopoly? On this board, the little pieces represented airplanes. The crew used them to keep track of which crafts were landing on the ship, which were taking off, and which were awaiting takeoff, as well as who had to do what to care for them all.

We had the opportunity to speak with representatives from different parts of the ship: communications specialists, engineers, technology specialists, medical staff, chefs, air traffic controllers, public affairs and protocol specialists. Everyone we met was doing important work, and each individual was articulate and enthusiastic in explaining his or her role. From some of the officers, we learned that the ship had stopped in Spain because it was about to be deployed. The crewmembers never told us exactly *where* it was going. That was a military secret. But many ships that deployed to the Mediterranean, we learned, conducted their predeployment training off the coast of Cartagena. The naval secretary and the US ambassador would visit with the ships' crews to build morale, and often met with local officials to thank the Spanish military for their friendship and training assistance.

A few months later, Alan and I had the opportunity to visit another carrier as it was preparing to leave port. This time we arrived by air, flying in on a carrier onboard delivery, or COD—a military transport plane that lands on the deck of the ship to deliver supplies and passengers. On the COD, we wore all sorts of protective gear: helmets, goggles, jumpsuits, safety harnesses, earplugs. Our seats faced backward, and a shoulder harness strapped each of us in tight. With almost zero insulation, the plane was noisy, and there were only two small windows. I don't do very well with motion, so flying like this wasn't fun for me. And landing in a COD was even worse.

When a plane lands on a carrier, it clips into a large hook that pulls the plane back and brings it to a rapid halt. We received instruction on how to hold our bodies when we landed: put your arms across your chest, bury your head into your arms, and sit in something like a crash position. Our plane landed flawlessly—we touched down, I felt a big yank, we came to a halt, and that was it. I emerged unscathed, but my heart was pounding, and I had to take a moment to steady myself. It was exhilarating, but I was also scared witless.

"I will *never* land on an aircraft carrier again," I proclaimed to Alan. In fact, I did wind up doing it a second time during our stay in Spain—once again, I guess, proving the saying *Never say never.*

The only thing scarier than landing on an aircraft carrier, I found, was taking off again. We were catapulted forward with the help of the same hook that had stopped us, and as we left the deck, the plane dipped for a second. I was petrified. Were we going to make it airborne? I kept breathing and saying to myself, *You're going to be alright. You're going to be alright.* I had no idea if this was true.

Once in flight, we couldn't look out the window—there *was* no window where we were sitting. And we didn't bring any carry-on items such as books or iPads to distract us. The flight was basically ninety minutes of *When are we getting there? How much longer? I hope I'm going to be okay.*

I came away from my military visits with a newfound respect and understanding for the young men and women in uniform. Growing up,

I didn't have much direct contact with the military. My dad, who served in the US Navy, regaled us with a few favorite stories about learning to peel potatoes while working KP, or kitchen patrol. Beyond that, he never spoke much about his military experience. In the cultural milieu of 1960s New York City, military service was not universally popular. Friends and family of mine opposed the draft, the war in Vietnam, and the military-industrial complex in general. None of my friends voluntarily entered the service—that would have been unthinkable. Some of them, in fact, were die-hard pacifists.

I have always loved my country and acknowledged the need to defend it, but I had never thought much about the military or seen it as an attractive career option. I had little notion of what the everyday lives of soldiers and sailors were actually like. That changed quickly once I got to know about our military and the men and women who serve.

During my trips to US military facilities in Spain, I questioned servicemen and servicewomen about many things: Why had they enlisted? Why had they become officers? What did they hope to do with their lives? Why was the military meaningful to them? Their answers taught me that the military truly is an exciting career choice, one that offers opportunity for advancement and personal growth across many fields, from communications to engineering to information technology. These bright young men and women had dreams. They held cherished beliefs and principles. In the military, they found an opportunity to broaden their horizons and discover the world. Many had been stationed in different countries and had acquired new skills and expertise. All, of course, felt privileged to serve our country while also pursuing their own futures.

Travel, at its best, pushes you beyond yourself. Your experiences challenge your own parochial assumptions. You don't necessarily abandon your previous ways of thinking, but you do broaden them. I scarcely could have anticipated that living in a foreign country would allow me to understand and appreciate my own country's military services, but it did exactly that. I found that I had something in common with these American patriots who had joined the military: like me, they wanted to make the most of their innate gifts and give something back to the world.

※

OTHER EXPERIENCES I HAD WHILE traveling around Spain didn't so much challenge my assumptions as they did confirm them. Bullfighting and hunting, for instance, are both quintessentially Spanish pastimes with long and glorious histories. I experienced both, and while I respectfully acknowledged them as important parts of Spain's culture, I decided beyond a doubt that they were not "me." The color and pageantry were fascinating to behold, but with all due respect to my Spanish hosts, I simply could not take pleasure in the ritualized killing of innocent animals.

I saw my first bullfight in Sevilla, a beautiful city in Andalucía that is worth visiting for its own sake. In the twelfth and thirteenth centuries AD, Sevilla was the world's intellectual capital, a cosmopolitan place where Jewish scholars translated Greek philosophy into Arabic. They say that the Alcázar of Sevilla—the royal palace—was designed by Muslim architects and financed by Jewish merchants for Christian kings. Certainly, its Moorish decor is stunning.

During our visit, Sevilla was holding its traditional *feria* (fair), a week of festivities held on grounds a few kilometers out of town and attended by hundreds of thousands of people. Begun in 1847 as a livestock fair, the *feria* grew more elaborate and celebratory each year. Today, families, businesses, and organizations rent tents called *casetas* and spend the joyous time going on carriage rides, donning special attire, and savoring the festivities all through the night. The women wear traditional *flamenca* dresses, flamenco music drifts through the air, and the fair is alive with hospitality and celebration. While attending an event hosted by a gracious Spanish family, I danced flamenco in a *caseta* until two in the morning. At first, I had no idea what I was doing, but I did my best to follow, and the gin and tonics provided liquid courage.

I was also cajoled into attending one of the bullfights that are traditionally held during the *feria*. The bullfight ring in Sevilla is straight out of central casting. The stadium itself is white stucco on the outside, with interior walls painted deep pink and gold. The sand at my feet as I walked inside was a beautiful golden brown. We sat down on built-in concrete benches that stretched the length of the stadium.

As the action commenced, our Spanish friends offered color commentary, explaining that bullfighters are regarded as heroes in Spain, much as professional athletes are in the United States. They described the bullfight's three main parts: first, the *picadores* on horses emerge to taunt the bull; then, *banderilleros* poke the bull to further taunt it so that it loses strength; and finally, the matador performs the ritual slaying of the bull.

The matador engages in a dance of sorts with the bull, displaying boldness, machismo, and gymnastic skill. Spectators, meanwhile, cheer in specific ways and wave colored scarfs depending on the action that is taking place.

If my language is somewhat vague here, it's because much of what our Spanish hosts were saying was lost on me. Not wanting to offend anyone by how brutal I found the spectacle, I focused on the positive aspects of the performance. The fashionista in me will remark that I love the costumes the matadors wear: their ballet flats, their colorful and jeweled *bolero* jackets, their skin-tight pants. I also recognize the gracefulness of the matadors' movements.

Yet the fight itself struck me as unmistakably gruesome. These bulls were poked, prodded, and then slaughtered. Even with all the ritual nuances, it seemed senseless, and it was hard to watch a crowd cheering on all the violence and gore. To my horror, I discovered that if a bullfighter did a good job, he could cut off an ear as a prize—for a really good job, two ears. For an extraordinary job, he chops off the tail as well.

I wound up keeping my hands over my eyes most of the time. I tried to relax and remember that this was part of Spanish culture, but I didn't succeed. Apparently, I'm not alone. Bullfighting is controversial in modern Spain, and in 2010, the regional Cataluña parliament banned the pastime in Barcelona and throughout the region.

Hunting, from my perspective, was no better. In the spirit of trying all things Spanish, Alan and I traveled northwest to a small town near Salamanca to go partridge hunting. *Caza* is the Spanish word for "hunt," and like bullfighting, it is steeped in ancient, aristocratic tradition. Men wear sports jackets and ties, women wear blazers, and almost everyone wears a fedora-type hat—a far cry from the camouflage and neon ensembles popular in America.

The hunting site we visited was a rustic camp, with wooden cabins dotting the brown, scruffy hillsides. We were given a cabin of our own, which was pretty bare—just a bed and a bathroom. The thirty or so people in our party all gathered at a communal hall for meals, which were formal affairs at odds with the surroundings. At dinner the first night, we ate and ate—lots of meat, as one might expect. Breakfast early the next morning was also a cardiologist's nightmare: eggs, bacon, sausage, and ham.

After breakfast, we went further into the countryside, split into small groups, and took up positions among the rolling hills. We hunted alongside a handful of our friends, and were attended to by a few assistants, including a young man whose job it was to load our guns and hand them to us. As the guns were readied, dogs clamored off into the woods to scuffle up the partridges, prompting them to fly into the sky.

Boom! Boom! Boom!

I watched the first partridge get hit and saw its feathers burst apart. *I can't watch this,* I thought. *I'm out of here.* Yet I did stay, doing my best to avert my gaze.

Alan, however, loved it and proved to be quite a good shot. Because of my husband, there are twenty-four fewer partridges in the world today. He agreed to a second trip to hunt wild boar.

This time, I stayed behind at the main house and hiked with a few Spanish women who also didn't care for the sport. It was a gorgeous day, and we set off on a two-hour expedition, talking about everything from raising kids to the craziness of hunting. The Spanish women peppered me with questions about our life in America, and I asked similar questions about their lives in Spain. As we hiked down the trail, I felt an unexpected sense of connection with these women. We laughed. We smiled. We shared stories. It was really special.

When the hunters returned, they displayed all the wild boar they had killed. It was quite an impressive day's work. I didn't want to count, but trust me when I say there were a lot. The dead animals all got sent to a *matadero* (slaughterhouse), where the carcasses were readied for sale to butchers across Europe. I took comfort in knowing that at least these animals would be consumed, and their remains not just preserved as a taxidermic trophy on someone's wall.

My friends back home in America knew that bullfights and hunting would make me uncomfortable, and they had urged me to skip these events. But as I saw it, I had no choice. I was in Spain in an official capacity, to help my country create a deeper connection with our Spanish allies. The last thing I wanted was to insult the culture. Part of my job was to understand all things Spanish, including bullfighting and hunting.

So I resolved to participate and put on a smile while doing it. I never communicated my true feelings for bullfighting and hunting with Spanish friends. "How do you like bullfighting?" they'd ask me.

"Oh, I just love the outfits the matadors wear. Spectacular!" I responded.

Diplomacy is about building bridges between people and cultures. Yet you don't have to see eye to eye with other people on everything. You can and should stay true to your own beliefs and principles, even as you show respect for how other people see the world. Bullfighting and hunting tested me, pushing me well out of my comfort zone. But these experiences reminded me of something important: it is possible to disagree with someone and see the world very differently from that person, and still find common ground and mutual respect.

We hear a lot these days about a "clash of civilizations." In our own country, we see intense polarization along class, race, and political lines. Yet different peoples don't have to clash. They can coexist in their differences. And the individuals who make up these dissimilar cultures can still spend time with one another and build strong friendships.

❦

AFTER OUR INVIGORATING AND INSPIRING trips on diplomatic business throughout Spain, from Jérez del Marquesado to the countryside of Andalucía, I pushed Alan to make time for some private trips for us—visits to other parts of Spain with no official duties scheduled. Given how hard he was working, certainly we were entitled to take *some* time off. He agreed.

We ventured to the Costa del Sol, spending a long weekend in the beautiful town of Marbella, where we stayed at the storied Marbella Club—once a favorite of celebrities and jetsetters. We sat on the beach and soaked in the Spanish sunshine. We also ventured into the mountains above Marbella to the beautiful *pueblo blanco* (white village) of Ronda.

We would take many other short trips like this, breaks in a life that really was quite hectic and demanding. Despite having a security team and a driver accompany us, we always found these to be great getaways. One of my favorite vacation spots was Mallorca, part of the Balearic Islands. Mallorca is a large island with some of the most beautiful waters, the bluest of blue. Once, we chartered a boat, and our "skipper" parked in a hidden cove where we walked up a hundred or so steps to a seafood restaurant. It was accessible only by boat, and its grills were powered by a portable generator. Two dishes in particular—the fresh-caught *gambas* (shrimp) and grilled paella—were out of this world. We toured the inland part of Mallorca and delighted in the area's distinct Tuscan influence. We spent ample time by the pool and read, took walks, and enjoyed leisurely lunches.

Alan and I wanted to visit dozens of other places in Spain, and we did the best we could to experience as many as we could. I loved every town and city I visited, and every historical site. Spain is a confederation of regions that, as the saying goes, is held together by a rope of sand. In other words, as I found out firsthand, all Spanish regions are distinctive and autonomous: The northwest country is lush and verdant—green everywhere, from the mountains to the sea. Near Madrid and the surrounding region of Castilla–La Mancha, the landscape is arid and brown. Just to the north of the city are the sometimes-snowcapped Sierra de Madrid mountains, and to the south are vast and fertile agricultural lands. Beyond that are the beautiful coasts. Of course, olive groves and vineyards are just about everywhere.

Spain is a larger country than one might think—about the size of Idaho and Utah combined. Thankfully, the high-speed trains connect almost all corners of this fantastic land, and you can travel to most places on a two-to-three-hour high-speed train ride or an hourlong flight. Wherever you go, you find relics of ancient castles and medieval churches dotting the landscape, conjuring up images of what once was. Thanks to my trips, both official and personal, I became somewhat of a mini maven when it comes to Spain, learning everything I could about the country. I also like to think that I achieved a harmony and communion with the country, finding new parts of myself in its culture, people, and landscape, while still remaining firmly in touch with the person I had always been.

There was one moment in particular when I felt close to Spain. In 2011, I took my daughter Stephanie to Extremadura, a province west of Madrid, near Portugal. This is probably Spain's least-developed area, a land of open, rolling countryside speckled with old Roman ruins. Stephanie and I stayed at a small countryside hotel. One clear, sunny morning, I got up earlier than Steph (which is not hard to do) and decided to take a walk.

Throwing on some clothes, I stepped outside and ambled down a dusty road. The desert landscape around me seemed similar to what you might find in Nevada: big boulders amid reddish-brown dirt cover, scattered with cactuses, tumbleweeds, and other perseverant vegetation. To my surprise, I came across a murky pond. Sitting down on the shore, I let myself become absorbed by the peacefulness of the place. I listened to birds sing, felt the sun on my skin, and was immensely grateful for my life.

After a few minutes of this bliss, I got up and walked back toward our hotel. A strange but comforting feeling washed over me—the sense that I'd been there before, that I was actually *from* that area. I felt a deep kinship and sense of belonging as I imagined myself an old Spanish woman, dressed in black and pushing a small cart with an ox beside it. It was as though I saw a vision of my own, true self.

I'm not a mystical thinker, but I am not closed to mystical possibilities, either. And in that moment, I knew for certain that if I did have a past life, I lived it in this exact area of Spain. Alan doesn't believe in past lives, so he finds my account a little silly. But that hasn't stopped me from recounting this little story to quite a few people. I know something happened to me that day. I've returned to that pond in Extremadura three times since. And back in America, I continue to think about it.

I uncovered a deeply submerged part of myself in Spain, far off the beaten path. And in some small but wonderful way, my life has never been the same.

THREE

FOODIE IN PARADISE

ASK ANYONE WHO KNOWS ME, and they'll tell you: as much as I love to travel, I love to eat even more. I am a foodie, plain and simple. I love going to new restaurants and trying new foods. I love going to different countries and eating *their* foods. I've eaten *bouillabaisse* in France, pasta in Italy, *pad thai* in Thailand, summer rolls in Vietnam, and *ceviche* in Peru—to name just a few. My adventurousness does have its limits, of course. If you said to me, "Tonight, we're going to have pig's knuckles and braised bug legs," I would say, "How interesting," and then offer a polite, "No, thank you." I'm a former-diplomat's wife, after all.

Still, I love experiencing a wide range of restaurants and foods, probably because I was raised with that tradition. In our home growing up, we reveled in New York City's diverse ethnic makeup. For us, Friday night was Italian, Saturday night was deli, and Sunday night was Chinese. On many of the other nights, we'd try great restaurants across the city. I loved them all.

I had long thought of Spain as a culinary mecca, a place a foodie like me just had to visit. I had clear, tasty memories of my visit to Spain in 1975: eating paella, strolling Las Ramblas while pulling olives out of a paper cone, starting my day with churros early in the morning. I even have some foggy memories of sangria-filled nights. Before Alan and I even knew where we would be assigned, I kept telling him that I wanted us to do a real, dedicated "food trip" to Spain. Instead of a food trip, of course, I now had over three years to experience and learn as much as I could about Spanish food and gourmet cuisine in general.

Spain has more Michelin-starred restaurants per capita than any other country in the world. It's especially known as a center for avant-garde, creative, "molecular" cooking. I was extremely curious about trying this cutting-edge cuisine, so I set myself a goal: during our three and a half years, I wanted to sample cuisine from all over the country, from street food and cafés to the very best restaurants. As far as the latter was concerned, I wanted to dine at as many Michelin-starred restaurants as possible. I succeeded in trying twenty-three out of thirty-four, or about two-thirds of them. Not too shabby.

※

MY CULINARY ADVENTURES IN SPAIN began almost as soon as we arrived. A month before we departed for Spain, Alan attended a dinner for the Spain–US Chamber of Commerce in New York, an organization that furthers economic ties between our two countries. At the dinner, he met José Andrés, the world-renowned chef, restaurateur, and humanitarian credited with bringing tapas, or "small plates," to the United States. José's restaurant empire began with Jaleo in Washington, DC, and has since expanded to other American cities including Los Angeles, Las Vegas, and Miami. Prior to meeting José, Alan and I had gone to Zaytinya, his other DC-based restaurant, which boasted a delicious menu inspired by Turkish and Lebanese dishes. Bruce Springsteen performed at a fundraising concert for Senator John Kerry as part of his presidential run in 2004, and after the concert there was a party at Zaytinya. While sampling hummus, falafel, and baby lamb chops in tzatziki sauce, we patiently waited to get a glimpse of the Boss up close. We never did.

On the evening of Alan's encounter with José in New York, they hit it off, and at the end of their conversation, José extended a gracious invitation: "When you and Susan arrive in Spain, please let me know!" People say things like this casually all the time, but it turned out that José was serious. Like most Spaniards, as we'd come to learn, he meant what he said. In late January 2010, a few weeks after we arrived in Madrid, José called us. "I'm going to be in Spain," he explained. "Would you and Susan like to join me at Madrid Fusion?"

Without knowing fully what Madrid Fusion was, I said I would love to go, even though Alan was unable to attend. It turned out to be an important gastronomy fair held in a very beautiful convention center called IFEMA. Attendance at this event is limited to just six hundred paying attendees. Die-hard foodie that I am, I couldn't wait. What could be better than visiting a food fair with a world-famous chef?

At the same time, this became an opportunity for me to attend an event in an official capacity, as it were. Since José was a Spanish native doing business in the United States, and the embassy's job was, in part, to help Spaniards conducting business in our country, I would be performing my first official duty as the ambassador's wife. Finally!

Embassies have "motor pools," a group of cars that drive senior embassy officials to work-related events. Since I wasn't an official employee, I normally didn't have access to this service, but because my attending Madrid Fusion was considered official business, I was driven to IFEMA in a motor pool car. I was the "official," sitting in the back seat, on the right side, just like Alan would. The convention center is a bit outside Madrid proper, so we spent an hour or so weaving through busy streets to the city's outskirts. When we arrived, José was waiting for me, and I was surprised to see camera bulbs flashing. At first, I thought they were there for me as an embassy representative, but it turned out they were the celebrity paparazzi, taking pictures of José.

America has its share of so-called celebrity chefs—Emeril Lagasse, Bobby Flay, Wolfgang Puck. I have my own favorites: Bostonians such as Gordon Hamersley, whose famous Hamersley's Bistro made the best garlic roast chicken *anywhere*. I also love Lydia Shire and Jody Adams, owners of great restaurants like Scampo (homemade mozzarella and pasta) and the former Rialto (wonderful fresh *branzino* fish and Tuscan steak). And let's not forget Michael Leviton, chef and former owner of Lumière, and Jasper White from Summer Shack and his incredible Essex fried clams. Yet in terms of their celebrity, these figures pale in comparison to Spanish chefs.

In Spain, top culinary figures are rock stars on par with Springsteen or Bono. Food and restaurants are a *big deal*. People do a lot of eating out, and they appreciate superstar chefs for their creativity. The chefs prepare innovative dishes, sometimes going so far as to rearrange the chemistry or the molecular structure of the food by infusing it with ingredients like cinnamon essence, nut paste, or just plain H_2O. In the arts, Spain is the country of Picasso and Goya. In literature, it has Cervantes and Lorca to offer. In food, it has artists like José Andrés and Ferrán Adria.

The media frenzy continued as we toured the gastronomy fair. Every few seconds, people approached to get a picture taken with José or to have him try their dishes. The event itself was incredible—an enormous convention center filled with booths and people shouting, *"Probad!"* (Come taste this!). The building pulsated with movement, aromas, and the sounds of people speaking numerous foreign languages. The food on display was truly global, making for quite an educational experience. In one area, we found a display of salts from around the world—black salt, red salt, salt from the Dead Sea, salt from the Mediterranean. Other tables featured dozens of olive oil varieties, or cheeses from around the world, or various kinds of seafood, or Iberian hams—more foods than I knew existed. If you think your local Whole Foods superstore has a great selection, you haven't seen anything.

As we made our way around, I soaked up as much of the culinary knowledge as I could understand. José, meanwhile, was in his element. He walks and talks very quickly—like a bundle of energy, very intense. He arrived knowing what he wanted to try and what he didn't. He was extremely kind to everybody, of course. He never said, "No, I'm not interested." He would take his time and speak with everyone who approached him.

At one point, as we stopped at a booth showcasing a variety of olive oils, he turned to me and said, "This vendor makes some of the best olive oils in all of Spain." He smelled the oils and had me taste them. As far as I could tell, they tasted like . . . olive oil. I couldn't appreciate the nuances. Yet José could explain in minute detail the differences between certain oils and even flavorings within the oils. He sampled just about everything at the fair, and I tried hard to keep up with the *jamón, chorizo* (spicy sausage), *salchichón* (sausage), olives, and *quesos*, and with all the small tapas I had never seen before.

When it came time to say goodbye, I thanked José profusely. Spending time with him had been such an extraordinary treat. As I was turning to go, he surprised me with another invitation: "Would you and Alan like to come to Oviedo with me for a weekend? I'll show you my hometown."

The answer was obvious. *Absolutely!*

A few weeks later, on a rainy Saturday morning, Alan and I (and the security team, of course) took the one-hour flight from Madrid to Oviedo, the capital of the northern region of Asturias. Once off the plane, we were escorted into one of those airport VIP waiting areas I was slowly becoming accustomed to. There we found José, welcoming us with open arms and a gleaming smile.

"Susan! Alan!" he called, clasping us in his arms. It was nice to hear something other than *Mr. Ambassador* and *Mrs. Solomont*. We had been in the country for only a few weeks, and already I was yearning for the sound of my own name. "Come," José continued. "I'm taking you to lunch at one of my favorite restaurants."

As we traveled along in Alan's official car, I took in the green meadows and rolling hills on this grey, drizzly day. Every once in a while, we encountered a house with a red-tiled roof and a herd of cows or a few roaming sheep out back. After forty-five minutes, the car pulled over before a small, nondescript stone building located just off the highway, just a few miles away from where José was raised. There was no signage, and the facility—whatever it was—appeared to be shuttered.

José jumped out of the car and led us to a small door at the building's front. He walked in, calling after us to follow. I glanced at Alan, perplexed, but he shrugged his shoulders, and we did as we were told.

We followed José up a flight of stairs and found something completely unexpected: a modern kitchen filled with glistening, restaurant-grade, stainless-steel appliances. Huge, expansive windows overlooked the countryside stretching out behind the building. Despite how the building had appeared from the road, the kitchen was enormous—probably thirty by forty feet.

The chef bounded out of a nearby office to greet us. Introducing himself as Gerardo, he welcomed us to his restaurant, established in this rambling stone house in 1882. Casa Gerardo was one of José's favorite restaurants, a place he had frequented for years. The two chefs greeted each other like old friends. Gerardo had been one of José's inspirations as a youth—in the kitchen, doing what he loved, cooking the freshest and highest-quality ingredients in simple but flavorful ways.

Gerardo escorted us up another staircase to a private, glass-enclosed dining area. Scarcely were we seated when he began bringing us course after course after course. The entire menu was in Spanish, so we relied on José to help us decipher it. He raved about the sea urchins, which arrived in a big bucket. If you've ever gone scuba diving or snorkeling, you know what these things look like, with their dark, porcupine-like shells. José demonstrated how to eat them: by cracking into the bottom and using a little spoon to scoop out the meat. As I said, I consider myself a fairly adventurous eater, but I was not *that* adventurous, and neither was Alan. We gave our portions over to José, who happily indulged after he'd finished his own.

Next, Gerardo and his staff served us several fish courses. We learned that fish was plentiful there, and that restaurants like Casa Gerardo served whatever was freshly caught that day. It is no exaggeration to say that the fish on our plates had been swimming in the cold Atlantic waters of the Bay of Biscay just hours earlier. And of course, we drank wine. Bottle after bottle after bottle.

This meal, which lasted for hours, was a revelation. I'd always thought of top-level restaurants as fancy places, with valet service and exquisite décor. This restaurant, which truly served world-class cuisine, was nothing like that. It didn't need all those showy, superfluous trappings. Everything we tasted reflected the honest, simple work of skilled artisans working with the finest local ingredients. In this out-of-the-way place, the food spoke for itself.

After we had stuffed ourselves, José drove us to our hotel, where I fell asleep in a haze of food and wine while Alan, of course, caught up on work. A few hours later, at about eight o'clock, our phone rang.

"Time to go out again!" José demanded cheerfully. He took us to our first *fútbol* (soccer) match, Gijon versus Barcelona. Team Barcelona, or "Barça" is one of the world's best. As we watched it live with José, he murmured constantly in our ears, explaining what was going on. In

Spain, *fútbol* is not just a sport. It's a religion, with fans maintaining near-spiritual devotion to their team.

When the rowdy game ended, we expected to return to our hotel and call it a night. José wouldn't hear of it. He took us to several *sidrerías*, restaurants were we drank *sidra*—hard apple cider poured from earthenware jugs. We were taught to drink it the traditional way: by picking up the jug, hoisting it over one's shoulders, and letting the cider flow out the spout and into one's mouth. *Jamón*, olives, and buckets of urchins kept appearing on the table. We ate everything (except the urchins) and drank the night away. By two in the morning, Alan and I finally decided it was time to go back to our hotel. José, with his boundless energy, continued for hours afterward.

The next morning, we somehow woke early enough to meet José in the hotel restaurant for breakfast. He introduced us to his favorite traditional Spanish breakfast food, *pan con tomate*. For this simple dish, you just take French bread, toast it, grate a tomato on top of it, and add a drizzle of olive oil and a dab of a high-quality sea salt, and you've got a delicious treat.

After breakfast, José walked us through Oviedo, proudly showing us his city. We passed by a bronze sculpture of Woody Allen, erected by the town after he filmed most of *Vicky Cristina Barcelona* there. Our host also introduced us to the town of Avilés where the *alcalde* (mayor) gave us a tour of the town's new performance center, one of Oscar Niemeyer's architectural masterpieces, which was under construction at the time.

It was another rainy day, and as we navigated the charming town in our rain boots, we lost track of time. Knowing we had to catch a flight back to Madrid, we called Enrique, our driver, to pick us up in the armored SUV. Enrique hadn't lost track of time. No matter where we were, our drivers and security team always waited patiently for us to be ready. As soon as we settled into the vehicle, Enrique guided us along the best route to the airport. Our drivers were expertly trained and very cautious about turning on the flashing lights and sirens used in motorcades. But this time we were late.

Suddenly hearing a noise, Alan leaned over to ask, "Is there a police car or fire engine around here?"

"No, sir," replied Enrique. "This is us going to the airport."

We made it there on time, entered the airport's VIP room, and then boarded the plane. The pilot asked Alan if he'd like to join him in the cockpit for the flight. Even in this post-9/11 world, Alan was able to join the pilots up front as they guided us back to the country's capital. We arrived in Madrid, exhausted and exhilarated by our unexpected trip.

I came away dazzled by just how much Spain has to offer—so many wonderful cities, towns, and villages, and so many of them, like Oviedo, unknown to the average American. Happily, I would have a chance to experience many of them through food. Another person might have connected with Spanish culture by visiting museums or delighting in the unique architecture. I loved those things, but the food resonated with me most strongly. For the next three years, I would connect with Spain the way a true Spaniard would: by eating my way through it.

☙

AS IT TURNED OUT, I didn't have to travel very far to immerse myself in Spain's culinary glories. They were right there for the taking in Madrid.

At the embassy, we were lucky enough to have two immensely talented chefs preparing food for us every day. Rosita specialized in traditional Spanish foods such as paella and *gazpacho*, and she prepared some non-Spanish foods as well, including vegetable lasagna, pizza, and soups. Our head chef, Gustavo, was more experimental. He had trained with Paco Roncero, one of Spain's leading chefs, and although he was comfortable with all culinary styles, he gravitated toward the molecular approach. He would make *tortilla española*, traditionally an egg-and-potato quiche, but with a twenty-first-century twist: served in a martini glass instead of on a plate, with caramelized onions, the potato element presented as foam, and the yolk running out at the top of the glass. At the table, when we mixed all these elements together in the glass, the onions and foam would heat the egg, causing it to cook slightly. It was just scrumptious.

Gustavo would also make something called "spherical olives" (*aceitunas esféricas*). They looked like olives served on a Chinese soupspoon, but when you put an olive in your mouth, it would *explode* with flavor. Gustavo's process was the key. He had taken olives, ground them up, weighed them using a triple beam scale, and then mixed them with different calcium carbonate compounds. In some mystical way, the outside of each little sphere would harden as they floated in salt water. In the end, they were vessels of liquid, which lacked the consistency of a traditional olive but tasted like the best olives you've ever eaten.

I never in my life thought I'd have a personal chef, let alone two. For me, this was heaven on earth. I didn't have to think about shopping lists or what we needed to stock up on. In the summer, when we grilled outside, the chefs would cut up vegetables and arrange meat on a platter. Alan would stand at the grill and cook the chicken, steak, lamb chops, or vegetables, and assemble them on a plate. After our meal, the staff would clean the grill until it sparkled. A great way to barbecue, isn't it?

Yet as fun as this was, at times I found all the service a little restricting. As in many homes, my kitchen had always been the heart of the house. I remember entering the kitchen once to make omelets for us on a Sunday morning. Carlos, our footman, ran in after us, saying, *"No, Señor Embajador. No, Señora. Déjeme hacerlo por usted!"* (Let me do it for you.) He led us back to our seats, poured us orange juice, and served us delicious scrambled eggs. That ended our brief foray into cooking.

Many people fantasize about having a personal chef, but believe it or not, one gets tired of being served all the time. Sometimes, it was a little uncomfortable; other times, I yearned to just do it myself. I was more than grateful to have Chef Rosita and Chef Gustavo and their delightful food. But I was also grateful when I got back to Massachusetts and could make myself an omelet on a Sunday morning.

✺

VENTURING OUTSIDE THE RESIDENCE, WE made additional culinary discoveries. Even though Alan and I were tremendously busy, we tried to carve out time to go to restaurants in Madrid—just the two of us. Alan had promised me that we would have "date night" at least once a week during our time in Spain, and he kept his promise.

I kept a running list of every delicious restaurant we tried, including those that served non-Spanish food. We loved a great Chinese restaurant, Tse Yang, down the street from our residence, and we ate there almost every Sunday; they remembered all of our favorites, including one of the best Peking ducks you'll find anywhere. We also loved El Jardín, the garden restaurant at the Ritz Hotel, where in warm weather we'd sit outdoors under a sunny sky, sipping gin and tonics while eating dinner. And just walking up the street to a tapas bar for some *pan con tomate, aceitunas* (olives), and *jamón iberico* was magical—the perfect Spanish night.

I made some gastronomic discoveries of my own in Madrid. One night in April of our first year, Alan was out of town, and I thought it might be fun to create a small, casual meal for myself. After weeks of eating in restaurants or enjoying the meals prepared by our chefs, I was prepared to take a stand and cook my own dinner.

Off I went to El Corte Inglés, Spain's largest department store—actually, Spain's *only* department store chain. The one closest to us featured a wonderful supermarket. I walked in and looked around, thinking it might be nice to buy some olives. Ten minutes later, I finally found them: a huge display of perhaps fifty kinds of olives on an enormous round table. The fact that this many olive varieties existed was both astounding and overwhelming. I wondered, *Which should I choose?*

I didn't want to ask for help, fearing that I would look like a total rookie. So I gave up on olives and ventured over to the cheese section. This was just as overwhelming: a dizzying variety of cheeses, located behind a counter, with an attendant who'd cut them for you. Mobilizing my shaky Spanish, I said hello and asked for some manchego. The attendant asked me a question in Spanish, which I didn't understand at first. She asked again, and then I realized: the glass case contained at least fifteen varieties of manchego.

Embarrassed, I retreated once more, mumbling, "*Lo siento . . . Hasta luego . . .*" (I'm sorry . . . See you later . . .)

I ventured over to a different aisle and wound up buying a large bag of potato chips made with Spanish olive oil. Back at the residence, Carlos the footman greeted me at the door. As always, he took my package, and when I showed him the chips, he said, "*Oh, Señora, me gustan las patatas fritas.*" (I like potato chips.) I gave him the bag and proceeded to have a glass or two of wine for dinner instead.

While totally unsuccessful, this shopping experience impressed upon me the sheer richness of the variety of foods in Spain. As a born-and-bred New Yorker, I like to think that I am anything but provincial, but food shopping in Spain was like nothing I had ever experienced. I made a mental note to ask someone, in the very near future, to take me to the supermarket and explain to me what I was buying and how to go about ordering.

Although I found the cultural differences inconvenient, on the whole I deeply admire Madrid's food culture, especially its emphasis on natural, local foods. The country's climate allows Spanish farmers to grow the perfect raw materials for culinary masterpieces. Both the hot, arid climate in the south and the rainier north provide ideal conditions for farming vegetables and raising livestock, and Spain's proximity to the sea spawns a great seafood industry. Almost everything they eat is local: the fish, the urchins, the cider, the wines. That, it seems to me, is the best way to eat. Why would you want anything other than the freshest food?

As I walked the streets of Madrid, I also came to appreciate the virtues of Spain's *social* orientation around food. In the United States, you often see people dining alone, grabbing sandwiches, or snacking at their desk. We are buried in our phones even when sitting across the table from our friends or family. In Spain, people go out together, walking the streets, sitting in cafés, and sharing food and wine. They gather in large groups in local restaurants, and we seldom saw them using cellphones.

Spain suffered a severe economic crisis during our time there, which left me puzzled. How could so many people still afford to go out Sunday afternoons for restaurant meals?

"Well," explained Ana Garcia, our Spanish teacher, "to save money, instead of ordering two gin and tonics when we go out to eat, we'll just have one."

Eating together in restaurants is an essential part of Spanish life. Food is a way of connecting, and not something to be sacrificed easily. I routinely saw multiple generations—grandmothers, grandfathers, aunts, uncles, cousins, parents, and children—all sitting together, eating, and enjoying one another's company. Even the residence staff at the embassy would enjoy meals together. Except for when they had official duties, they dined as a group just like the staff on *Downton Abbey*.

Another feature of Spanish food culture that interested me, and ultimately won my heart, was the frequency and timing of meals. Did you know the Spanish eat five meals a day? You have breakfast (*desayuno*) when you first wake up. You have a midmorning coffee and pastry (*almuerzo*), the *comida,* the big meal of the day, served around two or three in the afternoon. In the mid-afternoon, which falls around five p.m. Spanish time, you enjoy *la merienda* (an afternoon snack), followed a little later in the evening by *la cena,* or dinner, as the final meal of the day. And most Spaniards famously enjoy this meal at nine p.m. or later (but never earlier).

Due to our busy schedules, we often enjoyed an early evening hors d'oeuvre served with wine, *copita*. We loved *copitas*. Chef Gustavo positively spoiled us, making little sweet wafer biscuits, putting a piece of *foie* (liver) in between, and drizzling it with balsamic vinegar.

At first, this schedule was a little hard for Alan and me to get used to. As a matter of fact, Alan never got used to long lunches. "Lunch" for us meant gobbling a sandwich or salad in front of our computer at work. We weren't used to interrupting the flow of our day for a meal that lasted two hours or longer. Plus, it's hard for me to sit still for that long—even for food.

Ann Kreis, one of the first friends I made in Spain, picked me up one day to take me to Casa Benigna, her favorite paella restaurant. We got to the restaurant at one thirty and left around five. A three-and-a-half-hour lunch! By the time I got home, after all that rice and wine and good conversation, I just wanted to collapse in bed and take a long nap—not something I could do on a daily basis.

It took a while for both of us to grow at least somewhat accustomed to having lunch the way Spaniards do. After a while, it did feel nice to be invited to someone's house or a restaurant for lunch, and to feel comfortable sitting around for two hours in the middle of the day. In some ways, it brought me back to my own childhood. As a little girl going to P.S. 135 in Brooklyn, I walked to my grandmother's house for lunch every day from school, enjoying full-sized dishes like veal cutlet (on the bone), spaghetti, or roast chicken. Growing up, I hardly ate a sandwich. But that tradition ended in 1965 when I went to junior high school and it was too far to walk to my grandmother's house. Instead, I ate out with my friends almost every day: hamburgers, cheeseburgers, French fries, milkshakes, pizza—all consumed in thirty minutes. It's hard to imagine our fast-paced, urban society adjusting to a slow lunch eaten calmly and peacefully with family.

If lunch was awkward for us at first, so was dinner.

The first time we went out to a restaurant in Spain with friends, we arrived at five minutes before nine and the restaurant was still closed. It didn't open until nine p.m. sharp. By July 2013, when we came home to the United States, we *loved* dining later at night. To us, the hours between our normal dinner hour of six o'clock and the Spanish dinner hour of nine o'clock or later was found time. Suddenly, there were three extra hours in our day! We could go over emails, read the newspaper, take a walk, or sit at a café. Of course, that worked out in Spain because it stays light outside so late into the evening—as late as ten at night during the summer. Still, I must confess: Although we became accustomed to later dining, we were always the first people to show up at a restaurant, maybe at nine thirty or ten o'clock. We never fully transitioned to full-blooded Spanish dinners starting an hour before midnight.

※

MY CULINARY ADVENTURES IN MADRID and elsewhere in Spain opened for me a window into not only Spanish culture, but Spanish industry. In addition to olive oil, Spain also produces great wine, a staple in the country since Roman times. Spain has a great climate for growing grapes and devotes more land to wine production than any other country.

Over the centuries, the vineyards of many other European countries have been stricken by bug infestations and other woes, but Spain never suffered the same way, so it has become a great place to grow typical "European grapes." Another delicacy, as I've suggested, is Spanish ham, from pigs raised on the acorns of oak trees that are hundreds of years old. Acorns are filled with healthy omega-3 fats, and when these pigs consume them, their bodies become saturated with this healthy fat as well. If you have the real *Ibérico de bellota* from these pigs, you're eating something that's *really* healthy for you.

On one occasion, Alan and I visited COVAP, a farming cooperative that raises pigs and produces huge amounts of *jamón ibérico de bellota*. It was wonderful to see how lovingly the farmers cared for these animals. The pigs graze on pristine countryside, swelling to over six hundred pounds before meeting their fate. Before slaughtering them, the farmers bring them inside, give them baths, and play classical music. The pigs fall asleep, and only then are they killed. It is far different from the methods used in conventional, industrial slaughterhouses.

As we talked to the farmers, we found that they were unable to obtain approval to export their pigs to the United States. Apparently, what distinguishes an authentic Iberian pig is the black color of its toenails. Yet the US Department of Agriculture (USDA) frowns on animal imports to the United States with toenails intact. In the interests of fostering more trade between our two countries, Alan—as ambassador and our embassy's agricultural officer—helped the Spanish farmers navigate this regulation. Within the next few years, the Department of Agriculture will finally allow *jamón ibérico de bellota* to be imported into the United States. I, for one, will run to the nearest specialty store to buy it—if not for the fabulous flavor, then for all those healthy omega-3s.

Our efforts on behalf of food producers went in both directions across the Atlantic. In November 2010, representatives from the Alaskan salmon industry asked Alan and me to help encourage a broader distribution of salmon in Spain. I was really pleased when embassy staff, knowing how much I cared about food, turned to me for help on this venture. Working closely with our USDA section head, I organized a dinner to help "redefine" salmon for Spaniards. By that time, Alan and I had visited many restaurants as consumers, and we were able to invite several leading Spanish chefs over for dinner. One famous chef, Alberto Chicote, prepared dishes featuring American salmon. I loved that we could host our favorite chefs at "our home"—a wonderful opportunity.

My official involvement with Spanish food went well beyond specific industries or food products. I had the chance to highlight the importance of healthy, natural eating. Just as First Lady Michelle Obama had planted an organic garden at the White House, we planted one at the embassy with the help of a volunteer team. We worked closely with our USDA agent to organize it, and it became one of the embassy's popular community projects. Our agricultural officer, who handled environmental and energy issues, even created a catchment system for rain to irrigate the garden.

On Earth Day in April 2010, dozens of volunteers and their families assembled to help plant seeds and to learn about gardening. With Madrid's warm and sunny climate, and no deer around to eat what was growing, everything in the garden was ripe and ready for picking by late August. We invited the children of embassy staff, along with students from a local bilingual school, to harvest cucumbers; red, green, and yellow peppers; bright red cherry tomatoes; sweet lettuces; green beans; zucchinis; and juicy melons. Then we all went into the kitchen where Chef Gustavo helped the kids turn the produce into dishes like spaghetti made from zucchinis and gazpacho made from our garden tomatoes. I held up a big poster board that displayed different vegetables, where and how they grow, and what they're good for, to stress the importance of healthy eating.

On other occasions, I used my official role to cast light on some of the female entrepreneurs in the Spanish food industry. In June 2012, I organized an event on women in gastronomy, featuring Xandra Falcó, a leading wine and olive oil producer from the Marqués de Griñón vineyard; María José Huertas, the leading sommelier at Madrid-based Michelin-star restaurant Terraza de Casino; and an American expat living in Spain, Gabriella Ranelli de Aguirre, who leads gastronomy tours to unique places throughout Spain. In my opening remarks for the event, I began with an old Spanish proverb: *Con pan y vino, se anda el camino*, which translates to "With bread and wine, you can walk your road." In other words, with good food and wine, life is never too hard. As I went on to note, gastronomy is a field of contradictions: rooted in traditional practices and ideas yet also very contemporary, part of our day-to-day activities yet integral to world trade and globalization.

After these opening words, I moderated a lively discussion about Spanish food and the women who worked in the industry. More than one hundred Spanish business leaders, including top chefs and restaurant owners, had come to hear these three female culinary trailblazers. But as Chef Gustavo pointed out, we couldn't just *talk* about food. We had to eat! So before the conversation began, he set out some traditional Spanish foods: *pan con tomate*, *tortilla española*, sweet pastry rolls. Xandra Falcó served her olive oil, and it was indeed amazing. After an hour of mingling and tasting, we went into the residence's formal dining room, set up theater-style, to discuss why this topic was important and how these women had emerged as leaders in the field. I summoned my inner Oprah to conduct the interviews, probing how these three women developed their businesses, how they acquired expertise in their specialties, and what they were hoping to accomplish.

Events like this were especially important because they allowed me to form relationships with business leaders. In the culture of the US State Department, it has been more typical for the ambassador's wife to be invited to teas, brunches, and lunches with other spouses. Things are changing—but slowly. By creating this event and others like it, I was trying to show that I, too, had professional interests that could contribute to our diplomatic mission. It was rewarding to achieve a new visibility in Spain, and to help redefine what a diplomatic spouse could be.

※

WHEN ALAN AND I WEREN'T promoting Spanish or American food, or enjoying date night together in Madrid's culinary hotspots, we were— you guessed it—sampling more wonderful restaurants throughout the rest of Spain. The establishments we visited are too numerous for me to name, but some standouts include El Celler de Can Roca in Girona, Akelarre in San Sebastián, Moments in Barcelona, Santceloni in Madrid, Quique Dacosta in Denia, Arzak in San Sebastián, Azurmendi in Bilbao, and Calima in Marbella.

Let me describe a few of these very special places. No serious commentator on Spanish food could neglect Ferrán Adrià and his inimitable restaurant, El Bulli, which once ranked as the number one restaurant in the world. Open only six months of the year, and offering only one seating a night, it was the epitome of unique. The restaurant fielded over *two million* requests for reservations each year, but could accommodate only eight thousand lucky applicants. After Adrià decided to close his doors in 2013, he began a foundation for research and innovation in food and cooking. His legacy of culinary creativity can now live on for years to come.

In June 2010, my sister, Beth, and her husband, Jeff—foodies like me—came to celebrate her sixtieth birthday. Before Alan and I left for Spain, she had said, "Wouldn't it be great to go to El Bulli for my birthday?" Alan had perked up. "Well, here it is," he said. "My first challenge as ambassador. I'll see if we can get a reservation."

It wasn't easy, even for the US ambassador, but we managed to claim a spot on June 15, 2010, the restaurant's opening night of the season. As to how we secured that reservation—to this day, I am sworn to secrecy.

El Bulli was located in the town of Roses, about two hours northeast of Barcelona, on the rugged, mountainous coast of Costa Brava province. We visited Roses on a gorgeous, sunny, and warm afternoon, absorbing the breathtaking views of the Mediterranean Sea but also wincing as our large SUV made its way down a windy road with steep overhangs—a road designed for European racecar drivers.

Situated on the beach in a private cove, the restaurant was an elegantly but casually redesigned farmhouse. Adrià welcomed us into his immaculate kitchen, which was about the size of someone's home. In this high-tech laboratory, a kitchen staff of forty-two worked feverishly but in absolute synchrony. Staff and sous-chefs prepared and presented dishes to Adrià before he orchestrated their departure from the kitchen, like a great maestro conducting a symphony. The entire performance was, as Spaniards might say, *maravilloso!*

Dinner lasted from an unprecedented six in the evening until well after two a.m., and it consisted of no fewer than twenty-one courses of Adrià's amazing cuisine. The first six courses, the cocktails and starters, were served on the terrace. We moved inside for the remaining fifteen courses.

How can I describe it? There is a line in a Grateful Dead song: "The sky was yellow and the sun was blue." That is what Adrià's food was like. If you thought something was going to be hot, it turned out to be cold. If you thought something would be cold, it was actually piping hot. If something appeared to have a hard shell, its shell was soft. If something looked solid, with one touch of your fork it collapsed into a pool of liquid.

Take the first cocktail, a sloe gin fizz. Served in a small pilsner glass, the gin was topped by an inch-thick layer of foam. Expecting a cool refreshing drink, we toasted and sipped. But the cool gin came through a layer of warm foam, creating the perfect surprise.

My second favorite surprise was a peanut course. (Doesn't every meal include a peanut course?) Adrià's mimetic peanuts were part culinary delight, part magic routine—you bit into soft peanut shells, and warm peanut and chocolate filling oozed out. I liked them so much, I asked for an extra serving. I couldn't stop eating them. The expression "melts in your mouth" could've been invented to describe this delicacy. At El Bulli, nothing was what it appeared to be. It was dining as theater in a way I'd never experienced.

Another notable gastronomic experience occurred during a visit to the city of Burgos, located about two hours northeast of Madrid, in Castilla y León. My friend Ann asked me to accompany her on a visit to her husband's seventy-five-year-old Uncle Tasito and his lifelong best friend, Emilio. After touring the beautiful Burgos Cathedral, built in the thirteenth century, we drove with Uncle Tasito and Emilio into the surrounding hills, through beautiful countryside. Along the way, we spotted short, stocky vines, but no grapes growing on them and no signs of a building for making wine.

We puttered along windy back roads in the hills of Ribera del Duero until we stopped on a hillside for what appeared to be no reason at all. There were no buildings or vegetation nearby—just a door built right into the middle of a hillside.

Uncle Tasito got out, calling, "Come on!"

We followed him as he opened the door in the hill, and we stepped into an amazing underground cave. It had two rooms for sitting, cooking, and enjoying, and was attached to a cavern for aging and storing wine. No electricity. Dirt floor. Circular, wooden table with tree stumps for chairs. A wood burning stove, flickering. Dim lights hooked up by wires and car batteries.

Uncle Tasito and Emilio gave us a tour, and we hunched over as we walked through tunnels into a room filled with vats of fermenting wine. In this underground bodega, from grapes grown nearby, Uncle Tasito and Emilio made their own wine. Returning to the room with the wood-burning stove, we drank some of it. The cave was rather chilly, but the lamb chops and crawfish they grilled were stupendous, warming us right up.

We spent hours inside the cave, just as locals must have done for centuries. This unique dining environment reminded me of a line from another one of my favorite Grateful Dead songs—"I spent the night in Utah in a cave up in the hills"—except this cave is in Spain. I had no idea bodegas like this existed, and I never would have found it without a local resident to take me there. It was a truly authentic Spanish experience.

❧

I TAKE CONSIDERABLE PRIDE IN the fact that I lived in Spain for more than three years and gained no weight—well, not a lot of weight. All those restaurants, all those meals, and *all that wine,* and I came out relatively unscathed.

Today, there is so much about Spanish food that I miss: Chef Gustavo's baby lamb chops. Chef Rosi's pizzas made with corn and zucchini. The quiches. The paellas. They're just not the same anywhere else. I miss Spain's olives and its *lubina* fish (best cooked in a salt crust to keep it moist). There's a lot to miss. I honestly can't remember having a single bad meal in Spain.

Take away the actual food, though, and I've been happy to revert to American customs around eating. Since our return home, we eat dinner early again—seven thirty on weeknights, eight o'clock on weekends. And we make our own meals. As soon as we returned stateside, we hunkered down at home and cooked for ourselves. It is simply who we are.

We're not the only ones who grew to love the food in Spain. Our little dog Stella did too. Before we left for Spain, Stella spent most of her time with me. Once she discovered the kitchen at the residence and the cafeteria at the embassy, she started to hang out with the staff instead. She stayed with them each day, from the minute we came home from our morning walk until the time we left for her afternoon stroll. And unlike me, she put on about five pounds while there. For an eighteen-pound dog, that's a lot of weight.

On one occasion, we had guests over and were serving *jamón* for *copita*. When giving our friends a tour of the residence, we returned to find the *jamón* platter was gone. All the food on it, all the *jamón*—vanished. What could have happened?

And then I saw Stella, licking her lips. She had eaten it all—a foodie in paradise, just like us.

FOUR

"I'LL ALWAYS LOVE YOU"

THE PHONE AT THE RESIDENCE rang early one morning in late March 2010. The minute I heard Beth's voice, I knew something was wrong. Beth and I talked regularly, and I often regaled her with stories of my adventures throughout Spain and my plans for enjoying great restaurants together during her upcoming visit. But before my departure, we had made a deal: should any problems arise concerning our parents' health, she would call and tell me the honest truth.

Now she was calling to do exactly that.

"Daddy went into the hospital this morning," she said. "I don't think it's major. He just wasn't feeling well. He was having trouble breathing, but I think he'll be okay."

I thanked her for calling and slowly hung up the phone. A number of thoughts rushed through my brain: *Could this be it? Should I leave immediately for the United States?*

Beth had assured me that the situation didn't appear dire. My eighty-five-year-old father had been battling heart disease for some time, but he had always pulled through. I had no reason to think this time would be any different.

Hearing that my father wasn't doing well, an embassy colleague pulled me aside, saying, "I've been through this too. You might feel better if you went home to be with him."

I thought it over for hours, wanting to do the right thing. Eventually, I decided not to rush to New York quite yet. I loved my father dearly, but I didn't feel a pressing need to be with him in the hospital. For several years, whenever I spent time with him, I had prepared myself emotionally for his passing. Each time we parted, I told myself it might be the last, and said a heartfelt goodbye.

Several days passed. My father stayed in the hospital, but he didn't improve as Beth had thought. His breathing became more difficult as his lungs filled with fluid. He grew weaker and weaker. On Friday, March 26, I had just come in from walking Stella when I heard the phone ring. Somehow, I knew what had happened.

I went into the office of Cristina Álvarez, our residence manager, to take the call. "Hello?"

"He's gone," my mom replied.

My mother had a strange feeling very early that morning, so she went to the hospital earlier than usual. As she sat there holding my father's hand, he had smiled at her, just like he always did. And then he slipped away.

Cristina hugged me after I hung up the phone. I looked at her and said, "I need to go upstairs."

I went up to our private area to call Alan, who came down from his office within seconds. He took me in his arms as I cried. "Don't worry," he whispered.

Then the mundane details took over. Alan's administrative team kindly helped me make arrangements to get to New York for my father's funeral. I left the next day, Saturday morning, and Alan made plans to leave later that night. One hitch: our daughter Becca was in Morocco hiking the

Atlas Mountains, where there was no cell service. It took some doing to contact her with the news. With help from Alan's staff, she arranged to take a bus to Marrakech and then fly to Madrid. She met up with Alan there, and the two of them hopped on a plane back to New York.

We stayed in New York for four days. It was Passover, as fate would have it, so our extended family wound up celebrating the holiday together. "Isn't this just like Daddy?" we remarked to one another. "He'd want us all to be together." We brought in food, and my sister and her family, Alan and our family, and my mother enjoyed one another's company, joking and taking comfort. Although we felt the loneliness of my father's absence, we were grateful that we had each other.

On Wednesday, Beth and I traveled to Boston to sit *shiva* (a Jewish mourning custom) at her house. Afterward, I returned to New York to spend a few more days with my mom. As I prepared to return to Madrid, the most difficult part was leaving her in New York. She's not one to socialize much with other women her age. She's not a bridge player or a golfer. My parents had been together for sixty-three years. They were best friends for a lifetime, a single unit, and as my dad's health had declined, my mom had devoted herself to caring for him. My mother and father had found fulfillment in one another. I knew she had suffered an indescribable loss.

The loss for me was profound, and I was still struggling with a range of other issues. In ways I hadn't anticipated, living in Spain had distanced me from my family—physically, of course, but also emotionally. It placed new demands on my relationship with my mother as well as with our daughters. For the first time, Alan and I were not around to interact with our children daily, nor could I be there for my mother when she needed me. This distance made for some tough times and occasioned not a little soul-searching. But living in Spain also wound up bringing our family closer together in ways that, in the end, were both surprising and delightful. I managed to connect even more deeply than before with my role as a mother, daughter, and wife. As with so many of my experiences in Spain, my family became another area of richness that I could only discover as the ambassador's wife.

❦

I DON'T MEAN TO GLOSS over it: from the start, the new emotional distance I felt from my family pained me. Our first Thanksgiving in Spain, some six months after my father's passing, was also my mother's first Thanksgiving without him by her side. She asked if I would come home for the holiday, so she would be surrounded by family. I chose not to, and that was a painful decision to make.

Thanksgiving had always been the most important holiday in my family. Every year, my parents hosted Thanksgiving dinner and brought together four generations of our large family, from as far away as California and Florida. When I was a kid, my mother cooked the meal herself and served it at our home. It was quite a feast. But later on, when my parents moved to Manhattan, we couldn't fit all forty of us into their apartment, so we started renting hotel space in New York where nobody had to cook or clean. We would take over a banquet room and filled it with three or four big, round tables. There were also a kids' table and a table for gifts, because we used this occasion to celebrate the Jewish holiday of Hanukkah, which usually starts just a few days or weeks later. After dinner, the children would receive their presents—ripping open the wrapping, making an enormous mess of torn paper and boxes, and shrieking with joy over what they had received. It was wonderful and heartwarming to watch.

I had missed Thanksgiving only twice in my life: the year Alan and I got married and went on our honeymoon, and one earlier year when I lived in California. Now, my first year residing in Spain, I was missing it again. I had no intention of hurting my mother. I wanted to be there for her, and to help her feel a sense of familial warmth and togetherness even now that my father was gone. But I reasoned that my husband and I had been sent to Spain to do a job. If I was going to take on the role of ambassador's wife, I had to step into it fully.

Alan agreed. We had made a conscious decision to fulfill that commitment. I had to stand by Alan and to recognize that this was the life we were living together. We couldn't just leave whenever we wanted. We had duties to perform, and one of those duties was to share with our host country the most important American traditions and customs, including holidays. What more important holiday was there to share than Thanksgiving? It is purely American, laden with messages of warmth, friendship, and gratitude—a perfect holiday for achieving our purpose in Spain.

Once my decision was made, I threw myself into planning the embassy's Thanksgiving celebration. First, there was the guest list: we could seat only about a hundred people comfortably at the residence, and we had to figure out whom to invite. Then, of course, there was the menu. I had Chef Gustavo practice some of my mother's recipes, like sweet potatoes baked with mini-marshmallows. Gustavo said he knew how to cook a turkey, and he did not let us down. To feed one hundred people, he had to cook twenty of them, which took all the oven space we had. Each was succulent and delicious, earning our Spanish chef an A+.

El Día de Acción de Gracias, as the holiday is known in Spanish, was a great success—our guests all had a wonderful time. The residence staff deserved much of the praise. Decorated by Antonio, Carlos, and Byron, each table featured official State Department china embellished with the official American seal, and was decorated with maple leaves that Antonio spray-painted gold and many of the small glass objects Alan and I collect. I loved seeing them used this way, in a place setting that was simultaneously intimate and grand. The guest list included government officials, business leaders, and a growing list of personal friends. For many, this was their first American Thanksgiving celebration.

Alan offered some official remarks, welcoming everyone and talking about the beauty of gratitude. I also took the microphone and, in my best Spanish, thanked the staff for their hard work in cooking and preparing such a feast. All the staff members were supremely touched. They rarely received this kind of recognition, and they truly deserved it.

Standing near me, Adelina, head of the housekeeping team, started to tear up, until soon we were all misty-eyed. And to this day, whenever someone is a little teary, my family still uses the phrase *feeling a bit Adelina.*

✣

DURING THOSE FIRST THANKSGIVING FESTIVITIES and thereafter, I took comfort being in Spain, surrounded by Spanish people and culture. Spain is an incredibly family-oriented country. Most people don't live far from their families, as they do in the United States. Rather than move away, college students typically live at home and attend a university nearby. Many Spaniards rarely leave their hometown.

During the economic crisis that swept much of the country starting in 2008, the family remained the linchpin of Spanish society. Young adults who couldn't find work to support themselves moved back in with their parents. These parents also took care of their own, elderly parents in their homes.

Everywhere I looked, I saw evidence of how important large, extended families are in Spain. On the streets and in the parks of Madrid, we saw *generations* of family members spending time together—grandparents pushing young babies in carriages, adults sitting on park benches while young kids played in the grass. Older kids weren't going to the mall on a Saturday or Sunday afternoon with their friends; they were with family. We'd see fashionably dressed families out walking together in Retiro Park, the children in matching ensembles and wearing those little knee-highs with nice leather shoes—no sneakers or sweatshirts from the Gap! It brought back memories of my own youth when my grandmother made my clothing by hand. I'd wear the beautiful dresses she crafted, along with patent leather shoes and ruffled white socks, always doing my best not to dirty my outfit—but not always succeeding.

On several occasions, we were invited to join such families at homes outside Madrid. Some were grand country homes in the Spanish countryside, and others were more modest beach houses by the sea, but the close family bonds were the same. Once, we were invited to a friend's family home in Estepona, a small beach town in the south of Spain. The home had been her parents', and now she owns it. Her brothers, who live nearby, would come and eat almost every dinner together, along with their wives and children. Yet this was no mega-mansion. It was a true family home overlooking the Mediterranean Sea, with a nearby beach perfect for sunset strolls.

Experiences such as these transported me to my years growing up in 1950s Brooklyn. Back then, our family was every bit as close as the Spanish ones I encountered. We lived on East 48th Street and Lenox Road, and my grandmother lived two blocks away, on East 46th Street. In between those two homes lived a cousin who was my closest playmate throughout elementary school. Down the street lived my mother's sister. Her other sister lived upstairs from my grandmother.

Not a single Sunday went by without us visiting family members, sometimes piling into the car and driving to visit my father's sister in Jericho, Long Island. Getting together with family was just what we did. In addition to walking to my grandmother's home every day to eat lunch, I would end the day in a neighborhood playground, surrounded by close family friends. You didn't arrange a play date. Kids were just around, and you went outside and played while your parents and grand-parents sat on the porch and chatted. We played ball games. We rode bikes. We roller-skated. We roamed the streets after dinner without so much as a thought about safety.

Watching the Spanish live in a similar fashion helped me reconnect with parts of my youth, and thereby with my father. For that I felt grate-ful. Yet I also felt sad for our tremendous loss—of my father, certainly, but also of the family of my youth.

Like many American families, mine has drifted apart over the years. We live in different places and simply don't experience these daily connections. The older generation has died off. Aunts, uncles, and cousins have moved away to get married or pursue careers. In twenty-first-century America, most of us don't enjoy close, daily interactions with family members. We may enjoy the freedom to live where and how we want, but we miss what it's like to play outside under the watchful eyes of grandparents, or to share family meals at a large table. Extended family is a wonderful thing—and in Spain, I discovered how much I missed it.

☙

WHEN WE LEFT FOR SPAIN, I wasn't certain how our time there would impact our nuclear family. Becca was twenty-four years old, had recently graduated from Tufts University, and was about to start a job in the development department of Boston Medical Center. At nine-teen, Stephanie was in her first year at Lafayette College in Pennsylva-nia. So in some ways, we were all beginning new chapters in our lives, and we approached them in ways that reflected our personalities: Alan was enthralled with his new job and attacked it happily and ferociously. Stephanie was over the moon about going to college and making new friends, yet also sad not to have her parents close at hand. Becca was "freaked out" about our leaving. I was a little freaked out too. Of the four of us, my phase in life seemed the most undefined, and I wasn't exactly sure how I would handle the transition.

We knew that somehow, we would all have to find a way to stay strong and connected. We decided to focus on communication. As we were preparing to leave, Alan asked Becca what she needed in order to feel close to us while we were away.

"I'd like you to call me every day," Becca responded.

So we did. Every day for the three and a half years that we were in Spain, we called Becca. She had gone through college and several years of postcollege life without needing constant contact. She was already an independent woman, quite settled in life, with a job, an apartment, and good friends. Yet Becca craves order and stability, and daily phone contact was what she needed to feel as though Alan and I were there for her despite being thousands of miles away. Because we all decided to make time for this daily phone call, she never had to worry about where we were or whether we were okay—and vice versa.

At first, Alan would call Becca at around two in the afternoon Spanish time, or eight in the morning US time, catching her as she was on the bus to work. Then I would call her at the end of the day—eleven p.m. our time and five p.m. her time, as she was commuting home. Our daily conversations weren't always substantive; in fact, they were frequently short and simple: "Hi, how are you?"

"Good. How are you?"

"Good."

"Great. Talk to you tomorrow."

At other times, the discussion was more involved; but regardless of content or duration, Becca appreciated those calls. And we did too. I overcame my concerns about leaving Becca, because I trusted she'd be all right with this new routine.

Stephanie, on the other hand, was a freshman in college, and I worried about missing that experience. We did bring her to school and help move her into a dorm, and as our departure for Spain was delayed, we were still at home during her first semester. We attended parents' weekend and saw how she adjusted to her new life. But what would happen next? Would Steph have the support she needed? And how would I feel, being so far away from her?

I was surprised to find that in many ways, our time in Spain allowed us to connect with Stephanie and her college experience even more deeply than we might have thought. Every school break, Stephanie came to Madrid to visit us, always with friends in tow. Sometimes, she brought two friends, sometimes five, but she always traveled with an entourage. Because they lived with us for a week at a time, we got to know Stephanie's college friends. We'd start the day eating breakfast together. Then they'd go off on their own, and at the end of the day we'd regroup over dinner and they'd recount what they did and saw.

Their days didn't end with dinner. Spain is a late-night country, and at around one in the morning, the girls would go out to nightclubs in Madrid, not returning until four or five a.m. The next day, we would hear about the fun they had—or at least a censored version of it. If we hadn't moved to Spain, we would have visited Stephanie on parents' weekend and maybe another weekend during the year. We would have taken Stephanie and her friends to dinner once or twice, but we wouldn't have gotten to know them as well as we did in Madrid.

Both girls visited us four or five times a year for as little as a long weekend or, in Stephanie's case, as long as an entire summer break. Each summer, in fact, Stephanie worked at the embassy, taking advantage of a program for embassy employees' family members. Stephanie worked in the public affairs section, and when people asked her name, she answered, "Stephanie Sanchez." She did not want to be known as the ambassador's daughter. It was very important to her that she have her own identity, and I couldn't have been prouder. Neither did Becca draw attention to what her father did. She wanted to be "normal" and, like the rest of our family, unpretentious and accessible to others.

Whenever the girls visited, we enjoyed a great deal of time together. On one occasion, when Becca arrived with friends, Gustavo gave us a cooking lesson. When Stephanie visited, we roamed the streets of Madrid or took short jaunts to various regions of Spain. We also traveled as a family. One year, we went to Granada to explore the Alhambra. Another year, we toured a vineyard in Ribera del Duero. We traveled south to the region of Andalucía and *pueblos blancos* (white villages) like Ronda, and north to Cataluña and the city of Barcelona. When Becca ran the Berlin marathon, we cheered for her from the sidelines. We took a family cruise in the Baltic Sea, visiting the cities of Stockholm, Sweden; Tallinn, Estonia; St. Petersburg, Russia; and Copenhagen, Denmark.

Alan and I deeply valued our time with the kids, and we tried on each occasion to focus as much as possible on them. Having them around was an enormous comfort to me. Just taking a walk together or hanging out with them afforded me a wonderful feeling of normalcy. Conversely, my heart broke a bit every time the girls returned to the United States. I knew that they would be fine—that *we* would be fine. I knew we'd see each other during the next school or work vacation. I knew we'd talk regularly on the phone. Yet every time the girls left, I couldn't stop the tears. I missed them terribly when we weren't together. And nothing could change that.

※

WHEN ALAN WAS OFFERED THE ambassadorship, we knew it would affect our relationship in unpredictable ways. Without friends or family nearby, it would be just the two of us (along with Stella, of course!), and we would need to rely on one another in unfamiliar ways. Unlike my parents, who were inseparable, Alan and I had maintained a healthy degree of autonomy in our marriage. We were immersed in our own careers—Alan in business and politics, me in public broadcasting and philanthropy. Our marriage was happy, but we had never worked closely in a professional way. As we prepared to leave for Spain, we weren't certain how we would handle our new dependency and proximity.

I was excited for Alan, yet bereft at the prospect of leaving behind everything and everyone I knew. I didn't want to spoil Alan's own excitement, but what was I to do with my feelings? I couldn't just file them away. I had to let them out, and Alan needed a chance to react to them.

We decided to seek outside help, hoping to gain tools that would help us get through the tough transitions we would experience. Therapy wasn't something I alone wanted to do. Alan believed in it as well, having sought perhaps more therapy over the course of his life than I had, and he eagerly agreed to go with me.

We had done work on our marriage before, and the results had been very positive. This time around, we sought private counseling with an amazing therapist, David, who grasped our situation well—the challenge of moving to a new country, the difficulty of leaving friends and family, the imbalance of power within our relationship, the desire of each of us to make our own mark. Thanks to David's wisdom and insight, Alan and I came together as a couple, learning how to express more clearly what each partner needed from the other. Therapy sessions were a safe haven where Alan and I could express the very different emotions we were feeling.

After we moved to Spain, we checked in with David whenever we came home. Therapy helped Alan and me feel strong and connected, like a team. We learned how to really *listen* to one another during a disagreement instead of rushing to defend ourselves and prove the other person "wrong." Learning to listen is probably the single most important relationship skill I've ever developed, and is still a work in progress.

Even with the tools therapy gave us, navigating the challenges of life in Spain was not always easy. Sometimes tensions boiled over.

During our first spring in Madrid, I found that I enjoyed walking Stella along the calle Serrano each evening. Stella loved mingling with the other dogs, and she was a great social icebreaker. People on the street routinely stopped to ask, "*¿Es una perrita?*" (Is she a female dog?)

I would answer, "*Sí, es una perrita y es muy amable.*" (Yes, she is a female, and she is very friendly). But even as I window-shopped and struck up conversations, I gazed at people in the outdoor cafés. Everyone seemed to be enjoying the company of friends, and I felt lonely. I had not yet made friends to go out with, and there was no family nearby. I had given up my career, my interests, and it was hard not to wonder: *What am I doing here?*

I needed more time and wanted more attention from Alan. The next day, I asked him for it. "On Friday night," I told him, "I want you to leave work at six p.m. so we can walk up Serrano together, sit at a café with a glass of wine, eat olives, and watch the people go by."

Alan agreed, and I looked forward to our night out. But when Friday came, he didn't make it home by six, or six-thirty, or even seven. When he finally arrived after eight p.m., I was furious. He offered to go out despite having missed the prearranged date time, but I refused. Sequestering myself in our bedroom, I shouted, "I don't want to go out anymore! I asked you for one simple thing!"

He let me scream and yell, and then he declared, "We're going out. I am really sorry I was late. I had things I needed to attend to, but I promised you."

His remorse didn't mollify me. Still, he was quite firm in insisting we were going out. We strolled up the Castellana, still fighting, our voices raised. Tears streamed down my face, and I hid behind sunglasses even though the sun had already set. I typically try to be guarded when it comes to showing emotion publicly. Yet as always, our security team walked in front of and behind us. The poor guys were unwilling witnesses to the tears and the argument conducted in a language they barely understood—although perhaps they recognized such a universal language.

Over the next few days, Alan and I talked through our disagreement. For the first time, he understood how much more difficult it was for me in Spain than it was for him. Meanwhile, he relished every second even though his job required a 24/7 commitment. We both realized that to figure out how to lead our lives and simultaneously serve our country, I would need his help. And I wasn't used to asking for help.

During the months that followed, Alan learned to be there for me, right by my side. My father's death was a good example, as was an incident that occurred much later, during our third year abroad.

I had been working on a women's leadership initiative that was clearly in step with the embassy's work, when I received an especially disturbing phone call from a member of the embassy staff. This person rudely informed me that my initiative was "not a priority," and that embassy staff had no interest in working on it with me.

Whoa. Talk about cold water in my face.

I felt furious and humiliated. I was working my hardest to be helpful to the embassy, and this was how I was treated? At first, I was angry, but then my emotions collapsed into self-doubt and uncertainty.

Oh my God, I thought. *I'm getting no support. Who the hell am I? What am I doing here? And why am I doing this?* It was one of the most painful moments I experienced in Spain.

Although it was the middle of the afternoon, and I knew Alan was busy, I called him anyway. I remained composed—until I started recounting the earlier phone call. "I can't believe I'm being treated this way," I sobbed. "I would never talk like that. How could she be so insensitive?"

"Hang on," Alan said, "I'll be right there." He came down to the residence immediately and offered his full support. Hugging me, he whispered, "I'm so sorry. This is unacceptable. No one should treat you like that. How can I help?"

I was relieved and grateful to discover that he understood how I felt. His response had an enormous impact on our relationship.

As our months in Spain turned into years, I found that I, too, was able to be there for Alan in new ways. You know the saying *It's lonely at the top?* Well, it is. The State Department is hierarchical and quite formal in its protocol. Alan's senior team was a wonderful group of professionals, but they related to Alan with the formality and respect that the office of ambassador required. Even his most senior officers called him "Sir" or "Mr. Ambassador," never using his first name. He needed someone to whom he could open up, someone who would listen and offer honest feedback. That person was me.

Sometimes I found this role challenging. I treasured our time together as husband and wife, and I didn't want to spend all of it talking about the embassy. Nor did I want to hear about the excitement and challenge of his work at a time when my professional life felt somewhat empty. But I learned to listen to Alan's feelings and realize how hard he worked. Life wasn't always easy for him either, even if it seemed like a pretty sweet deal.

In addition to learning how to meet one another's emotional needs, an important secret to our success in Spain was making time to connect, indulge, and have fun. Much of Spanish commerce shuts down on weekends, and we were able to enjoy most Saturdays and Sundays together. We often hunkered down at home and just relaxed. Spanish television didn't appeal much to us, nor did the Armed Forces Television Network (AFN). So we survived on DVDs of American television that we received from friends. We watched *Modern Family* reruns for hours, and we lived for *Downton Abbey*.

We also used weekends to sightsee in Spain and beyond. As we approached one January weekend, I was particularly stir-crazy. Thankfully, we had planned a trip to the northwest province of Galicia. The day before we were scheduled to go, Alan came home and announced, "I'm exhausted. I need a weekend at home. Do you mind if we don't go to Galicia this weekend?"

I told him that I'd been stuck in the residence all week, and I felt housebound. I wanted to get out and do new things.

So what did we do? Whose needs won out?

In couples counseling, we learned that one way to resolve a conflict was to evaluate the relative importance of what each of us desired, on a scale of one to ten. On this occasion, Alan rated his desire to stay home as a seven. I rated my desire to go away as a nine. So we went to Galicia and ended up having a wonderful time.

One of the highlights of this trip was the magnificent Santiago de Compostela cathedral. We toured this UNESCO World Heritage Site from the rooftop. The cathedral is located on the pilgrimage trail of St. James, or the Camino de Santiago. According to tradition, St. James arrived in a sea scallop and brought Christianity to Spain. Symbols of scallop shells adorn the local architecture in commemoration. There are a number of different trails of varying length to walk on the Camino, some coming from France, some from different regions in Spain. People hike it for many reasons—some to find themselves, some as a religious or spiritual practice, and others simply for exercise. Walking the Camino is one of the few things I did not do while in Spain, and it is on my to-do list for when I return.

Another memorable part of the trip was Finisterre, where many pilgrims complete their journey along the St. James trail. Located at the tip of the Galician province, it is the westernmost point in all of Spain and continental Europe—a location that provides its name, which is Latin for "Land's End." The ancients believed the world ended here. It is an absolutely beautiful place, studded with road signs indicating how many kilometers you are from different places in the world. Alan hadn't wanted to leave the residence in Madrid—little did he know, we'd be venturing to the end of the world!

At home, it's too easy to find excuses to sit at your desk or attend to daily chores. Traveling took us away from it all, allowing Alan and I to reconnect with one another. We grew to love these weekend getaways, and we scheduled them as frequently as possible.

On some occasions, we visited friends who, like us, had the privilege to serve at other embassies. One January, we traveled to Vienna during the "ball season" to visit Ambassador Bill Eacho and his wife, Donna. The Eachos were wonderful hosts, and they arranged dance lessons so we could learn to waltz properly and dance the quadrille. We attended three glamorous balls in one weekend and enjoyed a wonderful taste of Vienna.

When we visited Stephanie, who was studying in Rome, we popped in on our friend Ambassador David Thorne and his wife, Rose. They lived in Villa Taverna—the second most beautiful diplomatic residence I've visited.

What was the first, you ask? Winfield House, the residence of the US ambassador to the Court of St. James in London, where we were the guests of Ambassador Lou Susman and his wife, Marge. That weekend at Winfield House was almost too good to be true. We also got to see an American football game abroad: the New England Patriots football team played the St. Louis Rams at Wembley Stadium. Heaven.

Besides weekend getaways, another practice that brought Alan and me closer together was regular date nights. When Alan and I first talked about moving to Spain and I began to express my fears, Alan made three promises: One, if we were miserable, we'd return home. Two, we would have a date night at least once a week. And three, when we got home to Massachusetts, we'd return to a relatively simple life.

Each promise addressed one of my fears. My fear of being unhappy was eased by Alan's reassurance that we *could* leave, if necessary. He would have been miserable if we packed it in, and I doubt I would have ever asked, but it was comforting to know that we were open to that option.

Date night spoke to my fear that Alan and I wouldn't have time for one another. We knew the position of ambassador came with a jam-packed schedule, and I worried that my workaholic husband could easily lose himself in the job at the expense of our marriage. Date night eased that concern. Each week, we looked at the calendar for a night that was relatively free of other commitments. Because of the necessary involvement of embassy staff and security, we chose in advance what we would do or where we would go. We were *religious* about keeping that promise.

When Alan and I went out in the States, we'd often go to dinner and the movies, or just get together with friends. In all our time in Spain, we saw only three or four movies, and we attended a few amazing concerts—Norah Jones, Leonard Cohen (twice), and a couple of Bruce Springsteen shows. Mostly, our date nights revolved around restaurants. We had endless fun exploring the culinary delights of Madrid and other cities we visited. When the protocol office called for reservations, security concerns prevented them from identifying the ambassador as the guest. But when they announced it was the US embassy calling, most restaurants figured it out. The restaurant manager always greeted us at the door and escorted us to a nice table, tucked away in a quiet corner.

Never having to wait for much of anything was yet another perk of this unique lifestyle.

When life got really busy (which was most of the time) and we just needed to get out, we took walks. On weekends, we loved Retiro Park, located in central Madrid, in the Salamanca *barrio* (neighborhood). The park stretches over three hundred acres and features stone paths lined with sculptures and statues, a magnificent Palacio Cristal (Glass Palace), and a small lake with rowboats for hire. On weekends, the park teems with families and visitors, but Alan and I felt very comfortable talking privately and walking with Stella off the leash. We'd review the past week, look forward to the next, and talk about the kids. Normal stuff. Now and again, we'd discuss a problem we faced, but mostly date nights (and days) were not for that. We just wanted to relax, have fun, and laugh. We treasured our time together, just the two of us: partners and best friends.

※

ONE OF AN AMBASSADOR'S JOBS is to showcase American values, and one of Alan's priorities was to highlight the great American tradition of community service and volunteering. Volunteering is not very common in Spain. Historically, the government and the Catholic Church have been able to address most human needs and provide most social services. Since the economic crisis, however, Spaniards have become more aware of the limits of these institutions. Ordinary citizens are being called upon to roll up their sleeves to volunteer, and I was very proud that the US embassy sought to encourage this trend.

When Alan first decided to make this a priority, he asked me to take a leadership role in launching a volunteer effort at the embassy. I gladly accepted. Working with US foreign service personnel and locally employed staff, I assembled a committee, and together we developed a mission statement and drew up a project list. We called ourselves Volunteers in Action (VIA), and we gained momentum quickly.

VIA volunteered to deliver donated foods to soup kitchens throughout the city, helped tutor immigrant children in English, and delivered toys to the young children of incarcerated women at a local prison. One Thanksgiving season, we collected over 550 pounds of donated food and delivered it to Our Lady of Mercy, a church in Madrid that serves a large Nigerian immigrant population. The following month, we partnered with the American Club of Madrid, our US Marines detachment, and the entire embassy community to collect toys for needy children in Madrid. About thirty volunteers, accompanied by two marines in formal uniform, then delivered more than 150 toys to boys and girls who were spending the holiday season in the hospital. Most of the families and children we met wanted their photos taken with those handsome marines—much to the ambassador's dismay! Alan joked that this was the last time we'd be traveling with *them*.

Of course, that's not true at all. We would travel with the marines any time. And VIA continues to thrive to this day, thanks to local Spanish staff who have committed themselves to the cause.

The organic vegetable garden we built on the embassy's grounds was our very first volunteer project, a collaboration between the VIA and other embassy sections. In April 2010, shortly after I returned from my father's funeral, we held an Earth Day celebration to launch the garden. It was cold, grey, and drizzly—unusual for springtime in Madrid. About thirty embassy employees showed up with their families, along with my niece, Amy, and our friends Tom and Marsha who were visiting us. The embassy's community liaison officer, Sarah Genton—whose job is to support family members of the embassy staff and help us organize embassy community events—played guitar and, along with her husband

Tom, the head of the public affairs section, led a singalong that included my personal favorite: "The Garden Song," by John Denver, with the lyrics, "Inch by inch, row by row, gonna make this garden grow."

The adults went to work, preparing the soil and planting seeds. Alan and I got down on our hands and knees along with everyone else. With members of the press in attendance, we wanted to demonstrate how important it is to show respect for the environment and our planet. The children planted seedlings of their own in little cups so they could watch the plants grow at home.

We stopped after a bit so that I could welcome everyone and Alan could deliver some prepared remarks. He reminded everyone about the significance of having an organic garden on embassy grounds. Then he pulled out a small, two-by-six-inch plaque and held it up for me to see. Speechless, I looked over and saw my niece with tears in her eyes. Our friends were hugging one another, and of course it was hard for me not to get teary as well.

The inscription read: *This garden in memory of Leonard D. Lewis.*

My dad never gardened, but dedicating the garden to him made a great deal of sense, because he was the first environmentalist I ever knew. During my youth, my dad did all kinds of things to help safeguard the environment, decades before it was fashionable to do so. My sister and I learned from an early age to turn lights off, not to waste paper, not to litter, and most important, not to leave the water running. My dad would be proud to know that I've almost trained Alan to turn the water off when he brushes his teeth. He also would be proud—and more than a little incredulous—to know that a garden at the US embassy in Spain exists in his honor.

Most of all, he would be proud to know that his family is stronger today than ever. As I said in the eulogy at his funeral, "Nothing was more important to my father than family. For him, the family was the sun around which all the planets revolved." Happily, neither his death nor our time in Spain weakened our family—not in the least. Despite my early fears, our entire family emerged from our Spanish adventure enriched and stronger than ever.

My relationship with Alan grew enormously during the time we lived in Spain. We shared much more professionally than we ever had. We were surprised to learn that we could work together and support each other in ways we never imagined. We gained a deeper appreciation for our respective needs, becoming more compassionate and understanding with one another. Before our time in Spain, I criticized Alan frequently, especially for his tendency to work so much. Although I still complain, I also have taken new pride in Alan's career, and I can empathize with him when he becomes stressed out. We find ourselves talking our emotions through more than before, and spending more time just plain old enjoying one another and having fun.

Our extended family emerged stronger as well. Now that we've returned to the United States, everyone is thrilled to see us at family gatherings again, and they wrap us in what we lovingly refer to as "the warm embrace of home." Participation in the family Thanksgiving traditions picked up right where it left off. My mom, who is eighty-eight years old as of this writing, continues to preside. A number of family activities make the Thanksgiving weekend special: shopping on Black Friday, dinner with Beth and my brother-in-law, Jeff; a visit to the theater for a matinee. The weekend ends with a big lunch of leftovers at my mother's apartment. My father is dearly missed, but we still enjoy a fun, family-filled weekend in the city, just as we always did.

My dad remains a constant presence in my life. Not a day goes by when he doesn't enter my mind in some way. I still feel a pit in my stomach and a sense of emptiness when I remember the call I received in Madrid and my mother's words: *He's gone . . .* Yet we hold on to his legacy, the centerpiece of his life: a commitment to and love of family. And we continue to feel inspired by Spanish culture, which celebrates family and makes room, week in and week out, for family bonds to take root and grow.

The memory of my father, and our three and a half years living away from our daughters and extended family, recalls to me an old folk song my parents used to enjoy. Believe it or not, it comes from the Iberian Peninsula:

> *Time has come for me to leave you.*
> *Tis the moment for goodbye.*
> *Ah my sweet, we have to part now.*
> *Please brush your tears from those dear eyes.*
> *We have shared so much together.*
>
> *Tis not the end but a new start.*
> *Ah, my dear, I'll always love you.*
> *You'll be forever in my heart.*
> *Ah, my dear, I'll always love you.*
> *You'll be forever in my heart.*[1]

---

1   "Tell Me Why," Portuguese folk song.

FIVE

WE ALL HAVE
JEWISH BLOOD

IN LATE 2009, AFTER ALAN appeared before the Senate Foreign Relations Committee—but before his confirmation—the Spanish press began to run articles about him. Headlines informed readers about "the millionaire businessman" and "Jewish businessman" who would soon be arriving at the embassy. We understood that the label was not meant disparagingly, but only intended to invoke Alan's background as a businessperson who happened to come from a Jewish background. Still, the notion of Alan as "the Jewish millionaire" came as something of a surprise to us. Although we were not poor, we moved in diverse circles and didn't define ourselves as "millionaires." Alan and I both took pride in our Jewish identity, but we defined ourselves in many ways: as parents, friends, professionals, political activists, community members, fans of New England sports teams, and yes, as proud Jews. It seemed odd that others would single out our Jewishness and highlight that, along with our wealth, as the two most important things to know about us.

Alan and I resolved that our religious identity would not define us in Spain. He wanted to be known simply as the US ambassador, there with his wife to represent the United States in Spain—and, oh yes, we were Jewish as well. What I couldn't anticipate was how much meaning I would derive from being Jewish in Spain.

Throughout my life, my knowledge of Spanish Jewry had been confined to what I had read in books, which meant the Spanish Inquisition—a period in which Jews and Muslims were persecuted, killed, forced to convert to Christianity, or expelled from the country—was foremost in my mind. Yet I quickly realized that my sense of past and present was skewed. Jews and Muslims had lived in Spain for centuries before the expulsion, coexisting in relative harmony. This era was known as *La Convivencia* (The Coexistence), *La España de las Tres Culturas* (The Spain of Three Cultures).

It was as if the Spanish experienced an age of enlightenment several centuries earlier than the rest of Europe. Ultimately, the expulsion and the Inquisition represent significant and sad chapters in Spanish history. But they're not the whole story. There are brighter and inspiring parts too.

In the five centuries since the expulsion of religious minorities from the region, Jewish and Moorish communities have gradually returned, bringing their rich cultural traditions with them, reconstituting themselves within the larger socioreligious landscape of Spain. This reintegration is a work in progress, part of which we saw play out during our time there.

Today, approximately forty thousand Jews call Spain their home. Most come from North African countries like Morocco or South American nations like Argentina. They strive to create and maintain a vibrant cultural and religious life. They are small but determined communities with synagogues and historical sites. To my delight, the Madrilenian Jewish community embraced Alan and me, teaching us a great deal about Judaism during our time in Spain. I encountered new holidays and traditions, and I also experienced Judaism in a new way, with a different intensity.

Initially, the celebration of Jewish holidays in an unfamiliar place merely marked my distance from the comforts of home. Over time, though, these festivities allowed me to stay *connected* with home. Spanish celebrations were a rare moment in which Alan and I weren't cast as diplomats or people of "importance." As congregants in the intimate setting of the local temple in Madrid or a personal residence, we felt like part of a community. Religion thus became yet another area in which I could grow and develop, even as I parted with my career and took on the role of a diplomatic spouse.

※

IN RETROSPECT, MY SPIRITUAL EVOLUTION in Spain was the continuation of a process of learning that had already taken root in my life. Growing up, I felt strongly Jewish, even though I didn't know much about the liturgy. I was a "cultural Jew"—perhaps a textbook example of one. My family did not belong to a synagogue. There was simply the neighborhood *shul*, a building where adults worshiped and boys went for Jewish learning.

As a girl growing up in the late 1950s and early 1960s, I was not given much schooling in traditional religious matters. The boys went to Hebrew School; the girls did not. Every Tuesday and Thursday at 2:30 p.m., a half-hour before school ended for the day, our public-school teacher would say, "Would the boys going to Hebrew School line up? It's time to go!" That's how Jewish our neighborhood was—public-school teachers letting out half the class for religious instruction. The boys marched out of the classroom, and the girls all lingered behind. I can't say I was too unhappy about that!

When I was eight years old, my parents decided to send me to the local Jewish community center on Sundays for basic lessons—what you might call "Judaism light." We learned the basics about central Jewish holidays, prepared ourselves for future social occasions by learning to dance the hora, and dutifully recited the holy prayer of devotion known as the *S'hema*. I remember misbehaving quite a bit there. I was usually well-behaved, but when it came to that class, I brought coloring books, spinning tops, and jacks—a big no-no.

"Susan, if you want to play," the teacher would say, "go to the back of the room." And I actually would! I'm sure many others can identify with this early and uncharacteristic experience of irreverence during religious education and training.

We celebrated almost all religious holidays together at my grandparents' house—my mother and our family, her sisters and their husbands, my cousins, and my grandparents. My grandfather would initiate meals with the briefest of blessings over the wine, and then he'd say, "Let's eat!" Not much of a religious service. Nor did our sense of religious obligation prevent us from making a Christmas pilgrimage to Manhattan every year to see window decorations in the Fifth Avenue department stores. We rounded out the day with a movie and dinner at a nice New York restaurant.

Did I feel as though I was missing out on a deeper religious experience? Not at all. I felt whole as a Jewish child, not lacking for anything. I vaguely understood about the Torah and the Talmud and all these other Jewish practices and customs and traditions, but I didn't know what I didn't know. It wasn't until I met Alan that I gained some inkling of traditional Jewish observance.

I always believed I would marry someone Jewish, and like many others in that culture, I felt subtle pressure from my family to do so. When Alan and I started dating, I knew he was Jewish, but religion was never a focal point of our early relationship. We met in 1981, when I was twenty-six years old and working at WGBH, Boston's local public broadcasting station. Alan was thirty-one. It was a chance encounter at a Super Bowl party in Andover, Massachusetts, where we found ourselves sitting next to each other on the couch and struck up a conversation. One thing led to another, and he asked me out. I said yes, unaware that his family was more religious than mine—Orthodox, as I soon learned. One Saturday morning, I saw his parents walking hand in hand up Route 9 near my home, observing the prohibition of driving on Shabbat.

My religious suitability for Alan was put to the test the first time I went to his family's house for a Friday night Shabbat dinner. Arriving at his parents' lovely brick colonial home, I found his mother in the kitchen cooking chicken, roast beef, chicken soup, and six different vegetables. This scene conjured up memories of my own grandmother cooking for company, and impressed on me the idea that Jewish mothers were the same everywhere—always in the kitchen.

Alan and I had arrived for the dinner a few minutes late. Everyone was warm and welcoming, but I could tell his parents and three brothers were sizing me up. I busied myself by staring nervously at the box of kosher chocolates I had brought as a house gift and making small talk.

We assembled around a beautifully appointed table, adorned with china, crystal, and silver, and sang "Shalom Aleichem," a traditional Hebrew song welcoming the Sabbath. Although I sort of knew the words from my days at summer camp, I couldn't remember them enough to sing along with the family. Then Alan's mother lit the candles, and his father picked up the Kiddush cup to sing a blessing over the wine. When the blessing was over, everybody got up abruptly and disappeared from the room, leaving me sitting alone for a few minutes. I was a little puzzled by this, but I didn't think much of it.

Alan's father was the first to return. Happy to make conversation, I said, "Mr. Solomont, this is lovely."

He looked at me and smiled, but said nothing.

I knew he wore a hearing aid, so I said it louder: "Mr. Solomont, this is lovely!"

He just looked at me and smiled again.

By the third time, I practically shouted, *"Mr. Solomont, this is lovely!"*

This time, he put his finger to his lips as if to say, "Shhh."

After a few more minutes of awkward silence, Alan's brothers returned to the table and Alan's father finally spoke, reciting a blessing over the challah bread in the Hebrew language. After that, he turned to me and explained that after you say the Kiddush, it is customary to get up and wash your hands. You recite a blessing over the washing of the hands, and then you remain silent until the next blessing—the one over the challah bread—is recited.

I had never heard of that before. My belated education in Jewish ritual had begun.

Three years later, in November 1984, Alan and I were married. Alan's childhood rabbi wasn't available to officiate the ceremony, and we met only once (ostensibly for premarital counseling) with the rabbi who would marry us. As we assembled under the *chuppah* on that cold, rainy November day, I distinctly remember the rabbi beginning his remarks about "Steven and Susan."

He had mistaken my soon-to-be husband's name!

While this was certainly one of the most unfortunate gaffs one can make on such an occasion, the rabbi quickly recovered. He turned to God in prayer, reminding us that God would never forget our names. Most brides would have been mortified by the experience, as I'm certain some members of Alan's devout family were. But I didn't mind. For me, the rabbi's mistake underscored the differences in our religious upbringings: I had never been close enough to a religious leader for him to remember my name.

Despite our different backgrounds, Alan and I grew into our relationship together, developing similar ideas about how to integrate spirituality and religion into our lives. During the early years of our marriage, we attended Alan's familial Orthodox *shul* for holidays. While this was edifying in many ways, we began to seek our own congregation and develop our own ways to observe.

In Alan's family's *shul*, as is customary in the more Orthodox sects of Judaism, women and men were strictly segregated, with the women cordoned off behind a curtain and the men sitting on the first floor. Services took place strictly in Hebrew, and everyone seemed to know when to stand and sit on cue—everyone except for me. Although we were committed to maintaining Jewish customs, Alan and I decided that we would need to join the right temple *for us* and develop a practice that was meaningful *to us*.

A turning point came when Becca was ready to attend nursery school. We had heard that the temple near our home had an excellent preschool program. When Becca was "accepted" to the school, our affiliation with Temple Beth Elohim in Wellesley, Massachusetts, began. With the help of wonderful teachers who believed it's not just the *children* who need to learn about their religion, but also the parents, I began to discover more about Jewish ritual.

Like many parents with young children, I was active in the nursery school, serving on the board and assisting with various activities. With all due respect to the women and men who help with bake sales and car washes, those types of activities weren't my forte. I liked being on a board and doing things that board members do. I became the school's board treasurer and the coordinator of admissions, roles that mobilized my skill sets. One assignment led to another, and I was asked to join the temple's board of trustees. From there, I embarked on a more immersive and profound exploration of my heritage. Because adult education was a pillar of our temple community, I began taking classes, and I developed a more historically nuanced and substantive appreciation of the Jewish holidays. I enrolled in a Torah class that focused on textual matters and the relevance of individual scriptural passages for my daily life.

As our children grew, the temple became a true community for us. Friendships blossomed for our whole family, and Temple Beth Elohim developed into an integral part of our lives. I became more and more involved, taking on leadership roles for many projects. I helped spearhead a membership project, working together with members of the temple to determine how the synagogue could serve people of all ages all year long. This campaign bore rich fruit and helped make the temple an even more vibrant place. We developed a robust adult education program, a dynamic Hebrew school, and devoted social justice and community caring projects.

My most important "big project" was chairing the committee to organize construction of a new temple building. This work quickly became a true labor of love. And best of all: it was a communal effort through and through. Everybody pitched in to make the building happen. Our team raised a lot of money, worked with a fabulous architect, and galvanized the congregation in support of the project. Whenever a challenge arose, someone would say, "Come on, we can do this!" And we did. We kept pushing together.

After three years of planning, we broke ground on the new building in the fall of 2009, just before we left for Spain. Construction took about fifteen months, and our new temple officially opened right on schedule, on December 19, 2010. Instead of being there in person, however, I watched the opening ceremonies from my desk in Madrid, live-streaming on the internet.

Although I was unable to be in Wellesley that day, at least I didn't miss seeing the congregation's Torahs paraded from the old building into the new. What an architectural masterpiece our new temple is! Two-story glass windows in front and on the sides allow natural light and the beauty of nature to enter the sanctuary at all times. The light wood tones of the interior endow it with a golden appearance that makes everyone present feel welcome and a part of the community.

Watching those opening ceremonies, I cried. This was yet another major life milestone I had sacrificed for the sake of Alan's career. But another part of me couldn't help but laugh. After my early days of misbehaving in my Brooklyn Sunday school, chairing a project to build a new temple was not something I had *ever* imagined doing. Lo and behold, I was a leader in the Jewish community. After an inauspicious beginning, I had helped create something beautiful and enduring for my fellow Jews to enjoy.

☙

ANOTHER IMPORTANT SPIRITUAL MOMENT FOR me occurred a few months earlier, during the Jewish High Holidays in September 2010. Alan and I had been in Spain for roughly nine months when we were invited to celebrate the joyful holiday of Rosh Hashanah—the Jewish New Year in which Jews review our conduct over the past year and acknowledge our sins—in Madrid's main synagogue, a traditional Sephardic temple. As Alan's driver navigated the twists and turns of Madrid's roadways, I saw no signs announcing a temple nearby, as you might find in the United States. I wondered if we were even going in the right direction.

Finally, after driving down a small alley, off a street that's off a street that's off a street that's connected to a main road, our car pulled up next to a door in front of a fairly nondescript building. We were seeking Congregation Beth Yaacov on calle Balmes, the foremost Sephardic synagogue in Spain. Was this even a temple?

During the High Holidays in the United States, members of the congregation would be standing outside in their finest garb, ushering other members in, chatting in the sunshine or the rain, and waiting to enter. Here, there was nobody. We stepped inside an unmarked door where, at last, attendants warmly greeted us and escorted us further inside. Everyone was subjected to a tight security screening, where pockets and pocketbooks were emptied. Not us, however. A welcoming group greeted the ambassador, and then Alan and I were led in separate directions.

The synagogue was beautiful and grand on the inside, where congregants worshiped in traditional fashion: Alan was escorted to the very front, and I was ushered upstairs to a section designated for women. Thanks to Alan's Orthodox family, I was familiar enough with the practice. On this occasion, though, I couldn't help but think, *This is our first service together in Spain, and we're apart.*

Fortunately, I was seated next to several wonderful women, some of whom I had come to know over the past few months. The wife of the Israeli ambassador to Spain sat next to me, and we shared a good chuckle when she turned to me and said, "This is the first time I've been to a temple in over twenty-five years."

Much of the service was indecipherable to me. Sephardic service follows the ritual traditions of Jews from North Africa, and I had been raised Ashkenazi, following the traditions of Jews from Eastern Europe. Also, my Hebrew is basically nonexistent, and my Spanish, at that point, left much to be desired as well. Yet from my perch above the main seating area, I was delighted to watch as Alan received an *aliyah*—that is, he was called up to say a blessing as the Torah was read. This was the congregation's way of expressing how honored they were by his presence.

The next day, we tried another local option, attending services at a more liberal congregation called Bet-El. We had heard about these services through Bert Schader, an expat who had reached out with an invitation to our family even before our move to Spain was made public. Bert would ultimately connect us to Bet-El's Rabbi Mario Stofenmacher, his wife Nuria, and Pam Rolfe, an expat and leader in the community, who would all become dear friends. Unlike most Jewish congregations in the United States, congregation Bet-El didn't have a building of its own to call home. Instead, the congregation rented out function hall rooms in the basements of hotels. Dressed in our Rosh Hashanah finest, we took the elevator down to the basement level of one particular hotel, where our service was taking place. There, we found an intimate scene of worship: no more than two hundred people singing and chanting together. They were dressed informally—slacks and button-down shirts or T-shirts for the men, simple dress pants and blouses for the women. Some people were even wearing shorts.

As we took our seats somewhere in the middle of the crowd, the rabbi smiled at us and said, "I'd like to welcome Susan and Alan." Alan and I looked at each other and grinned, pleased that he had used our first names.

We settled in, finding yet again that most of the service was in either Spanish or Hebrew. I tried valiantly to follow along. When there was something especially important that the rabbi wanted us to understand, he sent over Al Goodman, a Madrid-based reporter for CNN who belonged to the congregation, to whisper the translation in our ears.

As the minutes ticked by, I reflected that in present-day Spain, out of a national population of 47 million, there are approximately forty thousand Jews. If this congregation was any indication, this tiny group of Jews in Spain truly *wanted* to be Jewish. While Temple Beth Elohim in Wellesley has a dedicated Jewish population, many Jews in the United States are more ambivalent. There are enough of us around, and sufficient understanding about Judaism in the general population, that for the most part, it is easy being Jewish. But in Spain, it wasn't so easy—you couldn't take it for granted. Living a Jewish life was a choice that you consciously made, that you continually reaffirmed, and to which you constantly recommitted yourself.

As I gazed around at my fellow worshippers, I felt deeply moved, impressed, and *proud*. Seated all around me were people who truly wanted to be there. Nobody's mother had forced him or her to attend. In this respect, what this congregation had created in this makeshift sanctuary was every bit as beautiful as what we had back home in our brand-new temple building.

All things considered, though, I really did miss being home for the High Holidays. Our Rabbi, Joel Sisenwine, always has a warm welcome and a big, bright, inviting smile. Our cantor, Jodi Sufrin, has an exquisite voice. And our fellow congregants always greet one another warmly. Neither our daughters nor my mother, who would often attend our services, were there with us. I wasn't able to enjoy the meaningful and touching service in a language I understood. Rather, we were in a nondescript basement in a hotel in Spain—not entirely alone, but still lonely.

Thank goodness we weren't at the very front of the room, like Alan at the Orthodox synagogue. About thirty minutes into the service, a pit formed in my stomach as I thought of home. Despite the fact that I normally don't cry in public, tears streamed down my face. Soon, I was crying quietly but uncontrollably, and worse, I was out of tissues.

Though I was never comfortable walking out of a room abruptly, I knew I had to seek refuge. I got up and left the area where the services were being held, breathing a sigh of relief as the ladies' room door shut behind me. Looking at myself in the mirror, I rinsed off my face, took some deep, calming breaths, and reminded myself that we wouldn't be in Spain forever.

As I was calming down, another woman entered—an attractive blonde who looked to be in her mid-forties. "Hi, I'm Karen," she said, holding out a packet of tissues. "I grew up in California, and I've lived in Spain for fifteen years. I know just how you feel."

I took the packet in my hand, pulled out a tissue, and handed the packet back to her. "Thank you."

"No, no. Keep the pack," Karen insisted. "You'll need them."

I took them and thanked her, explaining how taken aback I was by my tears—I had no idea how hard this day would be for me. She understood, and I melted. "I think you're going to be my friend," I said, and we laughed together.

Karen and I exchanged contact information, and I walked back into the synagogue feeling much better. It was a sweet moment that uplifted my spirits and reminded me of home.

I reentered the services, and as I sat down beside Alan, he put his arm around me and gave me a little squeeze. He was trying to comfort me, but the gesture only prompted me to start crying again. Soon I was using up all the tissues faster than I would have liked.

And then I heard Rabbi Mario call my name. He was asking me to come up to the *bimah* (the altar) for an *aliyah*. I hesitated, but sure enough, it wasn't Alan they were asking. They wanted me.

I was initially uncomfortable, but I knew I had to go up there. Despite my puffy eyes, I felt honored and grateful to be welcomed in this way. I nodded my head yes.

I took a deep breath to collect myself, but it didn't do much good—I continued to sob. As I walked toward the altar, a woman unclasped the *tallis* (prayer shawl) she was wearing and gave it to me. So there I was, standing up before all these people, my emotions and borrowed ritual adornments out in the open for all to see.

When I reached the front of the room, Rabbi Mario glanced at me and again welcomed me with "Susan," not "Mrs. Solomont." He gestured toward Alan and again welcomed him by his first name, too. For a few brief minutes, we were simply Susan and Alan, two souls seeking to worship and welcome in the Jewish New Year.

As Mario gave me a special blessing, I chanted the Hebrew prayers for the *aliyah*, incredulous that I was still crying in public. Yet in this more intimate service, among these kind, welcoming people, I decided that showing my emotions didn't matter. I wasn't here performing my role as a stately ambassador's wife. I was here as myself, and in that capacity, I could express my feelings authentically and unselfconsciously. It was okay to be vulnerable. It was okay to be Susan.

❈

THIS SMALL COMMUNITY WOULD BECOME a spiritual home for us during our years in Spain. We continued to experience and explore our Jewishness, and we came to appreciate the blessings of a Spanish-Jewish community. We developed deep and enduring bonds with families belonging to the Sephardic community, some of whom became our dearest friends in Spain. The Hatchwells and the Misrahis would welcome us to their homes for Shabbat or holiday dinners. It was interesting to experience the same traditions, some in Spanish, others in Hebrew, but all universally Jewish—the same prayers, the same beautiful dinner table, the same foods like chicken soup, challah, and roast chicken. Like the holidays of my youth, the Spanish equivalent were family affairs, bringing newborns and great-grandparents alike together in celebration.

That first year in Spain, we had planned to host a Passover Seder, but we had canceled because of my father's passing. The following year, as Passover was approaching, I realized that I had foolishly forgotten to bring my Seder plate with us from the United States. During

Passover, it is on the Seder plate that we place the symbolic foods eaten during this special meal. Mine was especially meaningful as it had originally belonged to my mother-in-law. I needed to find a Seder plate in Spain—I needed one on our table. A member of the local community had offered to put me in touch with her daughter, who might know where I could buy a Seder plate. During our phone call, the daughter said she would get back to me in a couple of days with information. She did get back to me, although not in the way I had anticipated. A couple of days later, what should arrive at the embassy but a beautiful Seder plate—a gift from her family.

Jewish people in Spain and the United States have Passover in common, as all Jews do. But many practices were different. On occasions when we celebrated holidays with local Jews, I eagerly exposed myself to new rituals, new melodies for prayers—even a new tradition called Mimouna. Growing up in the United States, I had never heard of Mimouna, a special day that marked the end of Passover. The tradition originated in Morocco as a way of connecting Jews with their non-Jewish neighbors.

Jews are forbidden from eating leavened bread on Passover, and they're also forbidden from owning it. An ingenious way around this prohibition, which still adhered to the letter if not the spirit of the law, was for Jews to bring the *chametz*, as the forbidden food is called, over to their non-Jewish neighbors for safekeeping. Then, during Mimouna, Jews would welcome in their neighbors to express gratitude, and everyone would eat sweets such as figs, dates, or grapes slathered in honey.

Alan and I attended several Mimouna celebrations during our first year in Spain. As we found, traditions varied from family to family. One dinner we attended was as elegant an affair as you could imagine. Everyone sat at the dining room table, and uniformed waitstaff served the dinner. On other occasions, the festivities were far more casual, with the hosts bringing in deli platters and everyone showing up in casual attire. But both styles of Mimouna dinner had the same warmth and festive feeling. The essence of Mimouna, we realized, was simply to bring people together. In this sense, Mimouna was very much in keeping with the norms and habits of Spanish culture.

Getting to know Mimouna brought us into closer spiritual communion with Spanish Jews. But perhaps the most intense moment of connection we experienced was when our adopted congregation finally found a permanent home. Whereas our congregation back home had built a beautiful new building from the ground up, our Spanish "home away from home" settled into a space on the ground floor of an apartment building. The rooms were basic, not ornate or even decorated. There was none of the stained glass or mahogany pulpits or full-length windows you often see in American synagogues. But that didn't matter. The space was large enough for members of the community to hold a Sunday school program for their kids, to host services every Friday night, and to house community service projects. For this small, dedicated community of Jews, it was a wonderful, warm, and inviting place.

The new synagogue was ready in January 2013, and the community held a formal ceremony to inaugurate it, just as our synagogue in Wellesley had done for its new space. On a cold, wintry night in Madrid, Alan's security team and driver brought us to the new temple location. As we exited the car, we were greeted by Bet-El community members and escorted into the building. The excitement was palpable, and unlike other times when we came for services, it was standing room only. The main room that was used as the "sanctuary" was set up theater-style, and our hosts brought us to the front row.

As the procession of the Torah scrolls entered the new sanctuary, Rabbi Mario called my name, just as he had during that first teary-eyed service. "Susan?"

I realized he was asking me to carry one of the scrolls. What a proud moment!

In some ways, participating in the procession meant even more to me than attending the opening ceremony of my home synagogue. Here I was, bearing witness to the creation of a new synagogue in the heart of Spain. Mindful of the Inquisition and other tragedies that have befallen the Jews in this country, I felt as though I was doing something historic, helping sustain and safeguard Spanish Judaism for future generations.

※

ALTHOUGH I LEARNED A GREAT deal from my connections with local Jews, I didn't just want to understand how Spanish Jews practiced in modern times. I wanted to learn more about the history of Judaism and its relationship with other Spanish religions. According to the US State Department, about three-quarters of Spaniards identified as Catholic at the time—that meant learning about Catholicism.

The first thing I discovered was that while some might think of Spain as a "Catholic country"—a place where the women all wear lace black mantillas on their head and go to church every morning and night—most of the population is not especially religious or traditional in orientation. The Catholic Church forbids abortion and gay marriage, yet both have been legal in Spain for many years. The secular state has rescinded most "blue laws," which historically prohibited the sale of items such as alcohol on Sundays. And while Spaniards observe many religious holidays (All Saint's Day instead of our Halloween, for instance), not everyone goes to church.

That's not to say Catholicism is not culturally important to the Spanish—it is. As I discovered when embarking on the embassy's volunteer efforts, the Spanish have long regarded the Catholic Church as one of the country's primary social services agencies, relying on it for homeless shelters, hospitals, and senior citizen centers. The church also retains a significant symbolic role in the realm of high diplomacy.

At the start of each year, the Spanish royal family hosts a reception for the diplomatic corps. Ambassadors from over 165 countries are invited to greet the king and queen and hear the king's New Year's greetings. Ambassadors are asked to enter the Throne Room, which is merely symbolic; the country transitioned to democracy in the 1970s, and Spanish royalty no longer sit on the thrones. To enter in an orderly manner, diplomats line up according to seniority—how many years they have served their countries as representatives to Spain. By our third year in Spain, Alan and I had progressed to the front row, number thirty or so. But in our first year, we were among the last to enter. And guess who enters first? The Papal Nuncio, as the ambassador of Vatican City is known. It doesn't matter how long he has been in the country; in this case, he had assumed his post around the same time we did. His priority ranking is an enduring testament to the country's historic ties to and special relationship with the Vatican and the church.

While many people learn about world religions in classes or seminars, we were lucky to get a closer view. Throughout our tour in Spain, as we performed our diplomatic roles, Alan and I routinely saw evidence of Catholicism's profound influence and witnessed Catholic observances of all kinds. Since many of the Spaniards we knew were Catholic, we were invited to events such as funerals, weddings, and communions, in which Catholic traditions were on full display. We also attended many celebrations that marked important Catholic holidays.

One of the most memorable of these holiday events was Semana Santa, a distinctively Spanish celebration that is bigger and grander than all others of its kind. Translated as "Holy Week," it covers the week in the Catholic faith that leads up to Easter Sunday, including Palm Sunday, Holy Thursday, and Good Friday. Although each locality commemorates Semana Santa in its own way, businesses throughout Spain shut down and offices close. For many people, this is often a big vacation week. Each town and city puts on parades and marches, reenacting Christ's last days and his resurrection. Usually, the observances are fairly somber, with participants dragging crosses and effigies through the streets. But one Semana Santa celebration we attended—and will never forget—was anything but somber. It was a joyous occasion, with music, singing, and one particular Hollywood movie star.

In April 2013, our good friends Javier and Arancha invited Alan and me to experience Semana Santa in Málaga, an Andalusian town located right on the Mediterranean's Costa del Sol. Javier and Arancha told us that their dear friend Antonio would join us for the festivities. After a two-and-a-half-hour ride on the high-speed train, Alan's security team picked us up and drove us to the port. Right there in the harbor, we watched a ship come in. Soldiers marched off, as did a baby goat in honor of the holiday—the goat was an enthusiastic participant in the parade. We then went down to the town square where we met Javier's childhood friend, Antonio.

Antonio Banderas, that is.

Originally from Málaga, he returns to his hometown each year during Semana Santa and participates in the town's celebration. That year, I stood in the front row during the formal procession, as the soldiers carried a replica of Jesus on the cross through the city streets, and the crowd sang songs in unison. And next to me stood this charming, extremely attractive actor, whispering explanations into my ear as various dignitaries passed by.

Be still, my heart! Every time Antonio whispered in my ear, I kept thinking, *Yes, keep whispering. There can definitely be more whispering.*

Antonio is just as handsome in person as he is in the movies. He is about 5 foot 8, very thin, and on that day, he wore a dark black suit, a white shirt, and a skinny black tie. He chanted each prayer and sang all the songs by heart. At one point, he pointed to a train trestle ten blocks away from where we stood. "When I was a boy," he told me, "I used to sit there and watch this procession, never thinking that one day I would be in the front row or be asked to help carry the cross."

Feeling the intensity of his emotion, I got a visceral sense of how deeply embedded Christianity is in Spanish life. It touches the people deeply and in unfathomable ways, even if they don't attend church regularly.

After the procession, we went to Javier and Arancha's seaside home for a Spanish lunch even bigger than usual in celebration of Semana Santa. Antonio came with us. I sat next to him, and throughout the meal, he was kind enough to offer explanations of the various dishes. We had fish for lunch, and for dessert, a traditional Easter dish called *torrijas*—like a *crème brûlée* French toast topped with cinnamon ice cream. It was so delicious that ever since then, I have made a practice of ordering *torrijas* every time I see it on the menu.

I sat there basking in the sun, eating my *torrijas* and hearing Antonio describe a film he was working on in which he would play Pablo Picasso. Picasso is also from Málaga, and this film was going to depict the creation of his famous painting *Guernica*. At that moment, I wanted to pinch myself and ask, *Is this really my life?*

※

AS WE LEARNED MORE ABOUT Catholicism, another central facet of religious life in Spain came to the fore, one that seems more relevant today. We often think of Spain as a country of religious intolerance, symbolized by the Inquisition. But while the Inquisition looms large in Spanish history, it took place over five hundred years ago. Following that unfortunate chapter, Spain remained a culturally homogenous country well into the twentieth century. After the death of the former Spanish dictator, Francisco Franco, in 1975, however, Spain began to experience a surge in immigration from North Africa, Eastern Europe, and Latin America.

More than five million immigrants moved to Spain during the economic boom. While Spain certainly faces the challenges of integrating these new arrivals, especially during periods of economic hardship, a great deal of tolerance, respect, and multiculturalism thrives in contemporary Spain.

Perhaps no experiences better alerted me to Spain's deeply rooted religious and cultural diversity than our visits to historical sites, most notably the Alcázar in Sevilla. The Alcázar is a large, castle-like building where Moorish royalty resided during the thirteenth century. The period between the eighth century, when Muslims arrived in the Iberian Peninsula, until the expulsion of Jews and Muslims in the fifteenth century is known as La Convivencia. During this time, followers of the three Abrahamic religions—Jews, Christians, and Muslims—lived in relative harmony. Traveling through Andalucía, we saw evidence of this harmonious historical era everywhere. While the architecture itself is stunning—the tiled walls, the decorative ceilings—a closer look at the hieroglyphic-like words scrawled on those tiles reveals writing in Hebrew, Arabic, and Latin. This period of peaceful coexistence, I began to understand, coincided with the golden age of cultural and intellectual dynamism in Spain. I couldn't help but wish we could experience a little more *convivencia* in our own day.

As Alan and I traveled, we looked for signs of Jewish history. We visited Sevilla and the Alcázar many times, each time coming away energized. It's true that Spanish localities such as Toledo, Córdoba, and Barcelona once served as a home for vibrant Jewish communities. Unfortunately, Jews no longer live in these cities. Some religious buildings originally inhabited by Jews have been restored to help explain what Jewish life was like in past centuries; others are no longer intact.

In Sevilla, we navigated the tiny streets of Barrio de la Judería, the city's Jewish Quarter, which today is home to a movement to recover Jewish life. In the library of a local university in Salamanca, we saw a Torah scroll dating to the medieval era, prior to the expulsion of Jews from the peninsula. And while there is no substantial Jewish population in Córdoba today, we saw its Jewish quarter—homey, quiet, and picturesque—with a beautiful sculpture of Maimonides, the medieval Sephardic philosopher and scholar. The Synagogue of Córdoba, located at the heart of this maze of small streets, doesn't function as a temple today, but remains an important historical site for the Jewish recovery movement as well as for Spanish Jewry in general.

Just two blocks from the Synagogue of Córdoba is my favorite site in the whole city: the Mezquita, a grand mosque dating from the eighth century. Inside, it has candy-cane-striped columns and intricate stone and marble work, and today it operates as a full-sized Christian cathedral. Córdoba was the center of Moorish Spain, arguably the cultural and intellectual capital of the world during Europe's inward-looking medieval period. At its height, Córdoba challenged Baghdad as Islam's cultural and intellectual capital. When Christians conquered the area, they found the Mezquita so beautiful that they couldn't bear to tear it down. Instead, they spared little expense on this wonderful mosque, electing to build a Gothic cathedral within it. Today, although the architecture boasts Islamic beauty—and the translated name of this landmark is the Mosque-Cathedral Monumental Site of Cordoba—it is technically the Cathedral of St. Mary of the Assumption.

In fact, at every turn—every significant location, every tourist attraction—I found evidence of religions respecting one another, of tolerance and acceptance that was once the norm. I say "once," but I would argue that it is largely the norm in Spain still today. As Alan and I interacted with Spaniards of every social and economic strata, we often encountered a powerful spirit of tolerance. That's not to say there is no anti-Semitism, but with only 40,000 Jews living in Spain today, ignorance and lack of exposure to the Jewish community is a bigger challenge. Perhaps because of the country's strong association with the Inquisition, many people think anti-Semitism is still rampant in Spain. But I would argue that Spain is more tolerant than the world gives it credit for.

On many occasions, Alan and I met non-Jewish Spanish men who had married Jewish women. We asked them what their families had thought when they brought home a Jewish mate. Without exception, they replied, "What do you think they said? I loved her; they loved her."

In general, Spaniards are open people—eager to engage with you, whatever your age, background, or nationality. This is a country where someone might meet you on the street and only moments later invite you to lunch. People are hospitable, and open-mindedness toward other ethnic or religious backgrounds flows from there.

As we traveled through Spain's varied regions, we talked openly with people about religious tolerance and respect. Alan and I were both interested in the topic, and it was one of Alan's top priorities as ambassador. During our time in Spain, we worked closely with US government leaders, including Hannah Rosenthal, special envoy for the Office to Monitor and Combat Anti-Semitism, and Farah Pandith, the Special Representative to Muslim Communities. In keeping with President Obama's commitment to this issue, we regularly attempted to bring members of diverse religious traditions together at the embassy, and to work with Hannah and Farah on interfaith initiatives of all sorts.

For instance, to commemorate the end of the Muslim holiday of Ramadan and the breaking of the daily fast, we held a special dinner called *Iftar* at the embassy, inviting Muslim leaders as well as representatives of other religious communities. During two of the three and a half years we were in Spain, Ramadan happened to coincide with the Jewish High Holidays, so we held a celebration for followers of each faith. These events were similar. A group of us sat around the table, eating the delicious, sweet food appropriate to the Jewish and Muslim holidays and talking openly about culture and religion. Guests remarked on the Muslim-themed art we'd hung on the walls. One photograph in particular, by an artist named Lalla Essaydi, showed four beautiful Muslim females—a young child, a girl, a young woman, and an older woman—in various stages of being cloaked. Writings from the Koran are superimposed over the images of the women. The photograph exquisitely depicts the struggle of Muslim women to achieve liberation. This magnificent piece invariably sparked discussion about religious differences and similarities.

On these and other occasions, Alan made sure the message of tolerance rang loud and clear. As he noted in one of his speeches, American presidents had long celebrated Iftar, starting with Thomas Jefferson, who hosted the Tunisian ambassador. In the wake of 9/11, George W. Bush made it an annual White House event. And Islam has a long history in the United States, going back to at least the eighteenth century. As I was surprised to hear, records show that half a dozen colonial soldiers with Islamic names fought in the Revolutionary War. Over the next two centuries, Islam became one of the fastest-growing religions in the United States, and it is now the country's third-largest religion. Sports figures such as Muhammad Ali and Kareem Abdul-Jabbar are American icons, and at least one Miss USA, Rima Fakih, has been Muslim.

Alan always emphasized Islam's rich contributions not just to the United States but also to Spain. After the Moors arrived from northern Africa in the eighth century, Spain experienced an early renaissance under Muslim rule. Córdoba became one of the world's largest and most important cities, with its gardens, university, and public libraries, not to mention the Mezquita and the Medina Azahara palace. Alan would point out that the glory of Muslim Spain is still evident throughout the country, especially in Andalucía, and that Muslims today contribute significantly to Spanish society. A good example is the work of Mohamed Chaib Akhdim, a member of the Cataluñan Parliament and founder of the Batuta Association, which assists recently arrived immigrants. As Alan once pointed out in a speech, "Muslims today are represented in business, government, and all walks of life in Spain." While Muslims do face discrimination in Spain, in general they are better integrated than in other European countries.

Alan earned many accolades for his ecumenical spirit. We made statements about tolerance and inclusion by holding and attending Jewish religious celebrations and encouraging non-Jews to attend. Every year, we went to an ecumenical Passover Seder held in a Catholic Church that told the story of the Last Supper and traced its origins to the Jewish Seder ritual. We also held a Rosh Hashanah dinner specifically for non-Jewish guests. After one of these dinners, Monica de Oriol, a dear friend and a powerful woman in Spain who hails from a prominent Basque family, sent a thank-you note with a special message that captures the spirit of multicultural understanding we tried to further with these events:

> Monday's dinner at the US embassy [offered the] warmest
> welcome. Many old friends [were able to] drink and chit-
> chat [while] seated at table, celebrating [this] Jewish-rich

tradition full of symbols of God's generosities. [When us]
Christians are invited to join the ambassador and Susan in
[the holiday's] profound spiritual meaning, some inner [part
of the] soul is touched. A big lesson is learned [as we] share
your beliefs, wishes, and fears. It is healing.

To Monica and others like her in Spain, I would say that it was not only your soul that was touched. Alan's soul and mine were touched as well, by Spain's acceptance of a Jewish ambassador and his wife, and by the general atmosphere of openness. No country is perfect, and I wouldn't claim that every member of a religious minority is comfortable in Spain at every minute. Spain faces the usual challenges in being a tolerant society, but it does a better job than the rest of the world might think. By and large, Spain and the United States share a strong and enduring tradition of religious diversity. During our time in Spain, Alan and I wanted to affirm diversity's value and to reach across the religious divide to celebrate our common humanity.

✻

THIS MISSION OF BRIDGING THE religious divide required that we not merely expose Spanish Catholics to Jewish traditions, but also familiarize American Jews with Spain. After we'd been in the country for eighteen months or so, we felt an urge to share our deep appreciation of Spanish Jewry with our dear American friends. The perfect opportunity arose in October 2011 when Rabbi Joel Sisenwine brought a group of sixty members from our temple in Massachusetts to visit Spain. The group toured Madrid, Córdoba, Sevilla, and Barcelona. We hosted a special Friday night Shabbat dinner at the residence along with members of Bet-El, our adopted Madrid congregation, and other Jewish friends.

This dinner was a high point of our time in Spain. We took care to seat Spaniards next to Americans, and at various points in the evening, we invited different members of both countries to light Shabbat candles or recite a blessing. How wonderful it was to see everybody from back home again, and to witness them interacting with our new friends! The food was wonderful too. Gustavo had learned how to make challah—a delicious ceremonial bread served on Jewish holidays, the Sabbath, or other special occasions—and our guests gobbled it up. He also learned how to make potato latkes for Hanukkah, which were quite good, as well as *sufganiyot*, little jelly donuts that I had never seen at Jewish holiday events before arriving in Spain. And, of course, we had wine and Oreos.

Oreos? Yes! When my daughters were in nursery school and I was learning how to make Shabbat enjoyable for the whole family, their teachers, Mimi and Laura, used to say, "Make Shabbat fun! Make it something that your kids will *want* to come to. Do something different! Put Oreos on the table, and start with Oreos. They'll love it." So I did just that, and the teachers were right—my kids did love them. So on this special evening, I put Oreos on all the banquet tables. I was especially happy that nursery school teachers Mimi and Laura were part of the temple contingent visiting us. When they saw the Oreos on the table, they started to cry. And that made me really happy.

Another emotional moment came at the end of the meal, when Jodi Sufrin, our cantor from back home, and her husband and fellow cantor, Roy Einhorn, brought out their guitars and started to sing a medley. We all tried to sing along to Leonard Cohen's "Hallelujah," even though we were a little tipsy and could barely remember the words. As we held hands and sang, I experienced a feeling of togetherness, like an enormous hug—all the more notable because these groups of American and Spanish Jews were meeting one another for the first time. It was a "kumbaya" moment—not in a trivial or cliché way, but authentically so: joyful and warm and unforgettable.

I expected that a visit from members of my home congregation would leave me homesick. Instead, it made me feel great. I had a chance to forge new friendships and deepen existing ones. Everyone was eager to learn more about Spain, and I was eager to teach. Once again, I wanted to pinch myself at the thought that I, a girl from Brooklyn, could serve as a translator between cultures, as a representative of the United States and, on this occasion, of Spain. On a deeper level, the trip was a healing moment for me—a moment when my permanent home merged with my adopted home.

What could be better than that?

҉

ALAN AND I CONTINUE TO stay in touch with many of our Jewish friends in Spain. We remain active from afar in our adopted synagogue there, and we have woven certain Spanish-Jewish elements, like the eating of *granadas* (pomegranates) during holidays, into our religious practice. We also remain committed to helping American Jews better understand Spain.

In May 2015, two years after the end of our tour in Spain, we led a group of American Jews from New England's chapter of the Anti-Defamation League on a visit. Over seven days, we combined "must see" attractions with sessions that gave participants different perspectives on the country. Spain's former economic secretary at the finance ministry, José Manuel Campa, addressed the group, informing them about the European and Spanish economies. We visited Casa de Sefarad, a government agency designed to strengthen ties to the Jewish community. Alan's successor as US ambassador to Spain,

James Costos, hosted a cocktail reception for our American friends and invited members of the Spanish-Jewish community as well. It was a great opportunity to have old friends meet new ones, and for Alan and me to return to our former Spanish home.

Everywhere we went during that trip, we talked to Spaniards about religious issues and their feelings about Judaism. At one point, a prominent Spaniard made a heartfelt remark: "We all have Jewish blood." It was a comment that laid bare a complicated past. During the Inquisition that began in 1478, many Spanish Jews were forced to flee the country or convert to Christianity, an entire community forced to abandon its culture. It's a tragedy that has reverberated through the centuries. Today, many Spaniards believe their family trees contain Jewish roots. This statement very quickly emerged as the theme of the trip. In our fractious and violent time, when extremism and fundamentalism crop up in every area of the globe, it's a message that bears serious reflection. Spain has been through a lot, but today, on the whole, the country has it better than most. I think back to some words Alan said to set the tone at one of our Iftar dinners. Acceptance of diversity is, he noted,

> *a value which is shared by Spain and the United States. It's the value most fundamental to American democracy and of which Americans are most proud. In today's world, which has been shrunk by the wonders of modern transportation and telecommunication but is increasingly polarized by fundamentalist thinking, this is also a matter of survival. It is only through interfaith dialogue and conversations that promote mutual understanding that we will find common ground and common interests. Our coexistence depends on this, and it is the only way for us to build a better future.*

I had always been open to other cultures and religions, and proud of the United States for welcoming everyone. But my experience in Spain helped me focus on diversity and religious coexistence while also deepening—and complicating—my connection with my own religion.

Upon our return to the United States, at the first Friday night service I attended in Temple Beth Elohim, I felt rooted in the present moment. I just wanted to savor it, to feel wrapped in the warm, golden embrace of the temple's dazzling main sanctuary. We have a wonderful thing happening here in Wellesley. We are Jews with a brand-new synagogue building; but far more important, we are Jews who sustain a warm, loving community. We are Jews who live in peace with our fellow Americans. We are Jews who truly care for one another.

That Friday night, however, I was a bit thunderstruck—partly because of the sheer comfort of home, and partly because I realized, sitting there, that you really can find "home" anywhere. I thought back to the Bet-El congregation, occupying space in a plain building in Madrid, and how proud Alan and I were to be there. That space was a spiritual home; the congregation packed so much value into those four walls. Seeing that, experiencing it, has helped me value my own temple even more.

I know today that Judaism is not fixed or stable for me. As solidly Jewish as I have always felt, my religious beliefs and engagement are a work in progress, something that has evolved and continues to evolve. It took going to Spain to recognize this. I went there as the wife of the "Jewish millionaire"—a term that still makes me uncomfortable. I returned home with a much richer, more complex sense of the person I am, of the people to whom I belong, and of my very notion of "home."

SIX

NOT YOUR AVERAGE HOSTESS

T HE EMBASSY STAFF MEMBERS WHO served with us in Spain probably won't soon forget Alan's surprise birthday party in 2012—the day the Wienermobile stopped by the embassy. Yes, the Oscar Mayer Wienermobile.

Knowing that my husband's favorite food is hot dogs, I had surprised him the previous two years at the embassy with some manner of hot dog celebration. This year, I needed to up the ante. Inspiration struck one day when I saw the Wienermobile winding its way through the streets of Madrid. I contacted the president of Campofrio, a Spanish company whose many brands include Oscar Mayer, and discovered that it was possible to rent the Wienermobile. The company was willing to put the vehicle at my disposal for just such a special event. Perfect! Now I just had to get it onto embassy grounds for the big surprise.

That was easier said than done. Every minute of Alan's day was filled, and many people had a hand in determining his schedule. I was doing my best to ensure that no one would whisk him away for work at the last moment before his surprise party.

I also had to keep Alan from noticing. Bringing any vehicle, not to mention this distinctively *unique* one, onto embassy grounds raised many security issues. It is hard to hide the Wienermobile because, well, it's a giant hot dog on wheels. Because of the way the embassy and residence are situated, I had to keep Alan confined to his office and away from the residence, so he wouldn't gaze out the window and spot the "guest of honor."

Initially, I wanted Alan to take a ride in the Wienermobile, but his security team said it was out of the question. So I worked with embassy staff to allow a stationary Wienermobile to be parked in the residence driveway. Let me tell you: the Wienermobile is beautiful. The hot dog is such a fabulous American symbol, as American as apple pie. Renting it for this occasion made for an awfully fun birthday celebration, and thanks to residence manager Cristina Álvarez and Luis Moreno, Alan's second-in-command, we were able to ensure that proper protocol was followed and precautions were taken. We had a full American-style picnic, with paper plates, cups, condiments, and of course, hot dog carts.

The biggest challenge of all was getting Alan out of his office. His staff assistant helped me concoct a story, telling Alan that I was giving an official speech at a local university, that I really wanted him to come, and that I needed transportation. His team even put it on his calendar. Embassy staff members congregated outside on our front lawn just minutes before we were set to depart for "my speech." The embassy and residence staff had a great time going inside the Wienermobile and posing for pictures. Meanwhile, I was waiting for Alan.

My husband is always late, and this day was no exception. At the appointed time, I rushed over to him, exclaiming, "We have to go! I have to give this speech. We're going to be late. Come on!" I tried very hard to keep him from looking out the window and seeing anything unusual. Luckily, this was easy to do. I just kept telling him, "Let's go, let's go, we can't be late."

Knowing what was waiting outside, I tried not to show my excitement. Alan was distracted and, to my relief, oblivious. As we opened the door, everyone shouted, "Surprise!"

He saw the Wienermobile and was shocked. On the lawn were 150 or so embassy employees. Music had been piped onto the grounds, and that children's tune was playing: *I know a weenie man, he owns a weenie stand.* Everybody sang out, wishing Alan a hearty, "Happy birthday!"

Despite it being February, it was another beautiful, sunny, sixty-five-degree day in Madrid. The outdoor air was delicious, and made even more delicious with the smell of good ol' American hot dogs. Everyone posed in front of the Wienermobile in a huge group photograph. I had fooled Alan for the third year in a row, and I was really proud of myself.

The Wienermobile was just one of many memorable events I orchestrated while living in Spain. When I arrived at the embassy, I knew that hosting events would be a big part of the job, and I was looking forward to it. I love socializing and have a lot of experience entertaining people both privately and in my work for WGBH and TPI. Seeing myself as a career woman, however, I chafed somewhat at the traditional wifely role of picking menus and hosting dinners and teas. For this reason, I initially found planning our special events a bit awkward. Soon, though, I came to love and embrace this part of being "the ambassador's wife." Hosting others turned out to be far more personally enriching, substantive, and frankly, fun than I had ever imagined.

※

I GOT MY FIRST TASTE of the formal dimensions of my role about two weeks after our arrival in Madrid, when Alan and I attended the annual ceremony at the Royal Palace. For the Spanish government to officially recognize Alan as America's ambassador, he had to present his credentials to the king of Spain. These credentials took the form of actual letters of accreditation: oversized documents signed by President Obama, printed on beautiful, firm parchment and encased in durable cardboard. Alan had carried the letters with us on the plane, protecting them as though they were the crown jewels. He refused to put them in a suitcase. Once we were onboard, he gently placed them on top of our stowed items in the overhead compartment.

On the morning of the ceremony, Alan donned a formal morning suit—an item for which we don't quite have an equivalent in the United States. We had to rent it at a store that specializes in formal wear for special occasions such as this. In the end, Alan resembled a character in a British sitcom, with a black morning coat with tails, white bow tie, a starched white shirt, a white cummerbund, and black striped pants with a satin stripe down the sides. Cristina Álvarez came with us to rent the suit. We listened to her speak rapid Spanish with the sales clerk as she cast her careful eye on elements of fit and quality that eluded me entirely. She made sure that the garments fit him perfectly, and that there were no blemishes or loose threads anywhere.

What was I going to wear? Good question. Originally, I was told that a full-length "daytime" black-tie dress or gown would be proper. I had zero idea what this meant, and was thankful when the embassy's protocol department informed me that it wasn't necessary. (Wouldn't it be nice if we all had a protocol department telling us exactly what to wear—and not to wear—when we go out?) I put on a beautiful knit dress instead. For me, unlike for Alan, this was clearly not such a serious and important occasion.

I was excited for Alan, but I didn't have any illusions about what was in store for me. During a meeting with the previous ambassador, a wonderful Texan named Eduardo Aguirre, Alan had asked what my role would be throughout the ceremony.

Eduardo had seemed confused. "Her role? She doesn't have a role. They put her in a room someplace. They give her some juice, some coffee. At the end, she meets you, and that's that." Alan was afraid to tell me this story, but eventually he did. And Eduardo was right—that's exactly what happened.

Meanwhile, Alan was transported in a horse-drawn carriage from the Spanish Ministry of Foreign Affairs to the Palacio Real, like Cinderella going to the ball. By contrast, I stood under a portico in the courtyard, watching as the palace gates opened and his horse-and-carriage procession passed through while a royal band dressed in eighteenth-century military clothing played "The Star-Spangled Banner." I could hear the clumping of the horses' hooves and the military band's sharp, moving notes as the procession came to a stop. The footmen opened the door, and out stepped Alan in his morning suit. He was joined by four other diplomats from the embassy and an escort from Spain's diplomatic corps.

As I stood there observing this very moving processional, I fought back tears. Just hearing our national anthem was poignant in and of itself. Add to that the pageantry of Alan's arrival in horse and carriage—it was a true "pinch me" moment.

The red carpet was unfurled on the palace's grand steps, and all the king's footmen stood at their posts. As Alan described to me later, he stepped up the grand staircase, passed through a series of palace rooms, and finally entered a room reserved for the presentation of diplomatic credentials. Awaiting him there, dressed in royal regalia was *el rey* (the king), Juan Carlos I, who at seventy-two years old was a tall and handsome man. Crowned king of Spain in 1975, he is beloved for leading the country through its transition to democracy. El Rey Juan Carlos is kind and affable and looked incredibly dashing in his royal clothing, with sashes crisscrossing his chest and military badges hanging.

Alan's entrance and the subsequent ceremony took place according to strict protocol. During our initial tour of the palace, we were shown how Alan would venture up the steps, how he would enter into one room, how he would then be escorted into the credentialing room, and so on. After the initial formalities, Alan and the king would spend fifteen to twenty minutes becoming acquainted with one another. In truth, the ceremony lasted a bit longer, because they really hit it off. Alan reminisced with the king about his initial trip to Spain in 1971 and how remarkably the country had transformed in the intervening period. The king seemed pleased by these comments, particularly because Alan accurately credited this transformation in no small part to the king's leadership and vision.

I watched Alan's entrance from the palace portico, trying unsuccessfully to record it on my camera. Then I was ushered into a rather unremarkable palace room where, just as Ambassador Aguirre had predicted, I was given orange juice and coffee along with a couple of other wives whose diplomat husbands from different countries were also presenting their credentials that day.

Although it was exciting and enthralling just to be there, it was also isolating. Despite the fair warning, I had still hoped that I would enjoy a little more pomp and circumstance. After all, this was my first official royal experience in Spain. To this day, it strikes me as odd and unfortunate that such ceremonies explicitly exclude spouses, partners, and family. I understand that they derive from eighteenth-century traditions, when such considerations were moot. But this ceremony took place in 2010, and society has evolved.

That night, Alan and I hosted a traditional reception at the embassy, celebrating the incoming ambassador. It was a fascinating evening, but also surreal and a bit of a blur. Hundreds of people crowded the official residence—our new home—wanting to say hello and get some face time with the new ambassador. Looking back on the guest list, I am somewhat amazed at the number and importance of the people who attended. From government officials and business leaders to socialites to longtime friends of the embassy, a whirl of people greeted us, welcomed us, and asked the same question so many would pose during our stay in Spain: "How do you like my country?"

With everyone crowding into our dining and living rooms, Alan gave his first public speech, conveying how pleased he was to be in Spain. I made the rounds on the arm of deputy chief of mission Arnold Chacon, who kept saying, "Mrs. Solomont, let me introduce you to so-and-so."

I can't remember meeting any person in particular that evening. I only remember everybody coming up and saying, "Welcome to our country. We hope you like it here. We're so glad to meet you. We love the United States, and we love President Obama."

By the end of the evening, I was exhausted. But I also noticed with pride how much Alan was loving his role. He was so poised and effortless on his feet, making important remarks and meeting people. He could have gone on all night. I was no slouch at these sorts of things either, but in comparison, I felt like a rookie.

During ambassador school, we learned that no one leaves a party or event until the ambassador exits. That evening, it wasn't easy getting Alan to leave and go upstairs. Maybe it's because women wear high heels, and by the end of the night, we're ready to get off our feet—or maybe I just knew when enough was enough. Either way, I was ready.

Finally, Alan and I retreated to our private quarters. We kicked off our shoes and requested that some of the evening's remaining food and wine be brought upstairs so we could finally eat, drink, and relax. Even at this early stage of our time in Spain, we were developing some fun rituals around entertaining—and this one in particular really stands out. After hosting a party, Alan and I would always go upstairs for some quiet time together. In later years, we'd invite a few embassy friends to join us at the "after party." But for now, it was just us.

❋

AS YOU CAN IMAGINE, ORGANIZING an embassy event—even a smaller, more modest one than our first official reception—was a *lot* of work. There was the food to think about, plus the drinks, the guest list, the entertainment, the speeches . . . the list went on and on. Fortunately, the full burden of entertaining did not fall squarely on my shoulders. Alan and I reaped the benefits of a wonderful and incredibly talented protocol team, three women who really understood the networks of people who made up Spanish society, including the political and business community, the art community, the socialite community, and the royal family. We owe an enormous debt to these three women, who have since become dear friends: Marta Soriano, Beatriz Agenjo, and Marta Peralta.

The protocol team helped us assemble guest lists, updated us about political relationships in the country, and briefed us on government officials—the minister of finance, the minister of the interior, the minister of the environment and agriculture, the minister of defense. Others in the embassy, such as Alan's political team, sometimes helped us plan events. Members of the public affairs department also planned certain events and often helped us understand if the guest list was incomplete—or if there was anyone whom we shouldn't invite.

All of our entertaining took place on an extremely slim budget, which posed an additional logistical challenge. Americans would be wrong to think that diplomats are spending hard-earned tax dollars on lavish embassy parties. On the contrary, we were very judicious about the events we hosted, making sure they all served an important purpose related to embassy business. Our chefs, Gustavo and Rosi, carefully planned our menus, always bearing in mind the food and beverage costs. As we lacked a budget for incidentals, such as flowers for table centerpieces, our talented residence staff picked flowers from the garden or selected glass objects or ceramic pieces that Alan and I had brought with us from the United States.

Alan and I both collect odd and sundry items. He likes spoons from different cities, towns, and countries we visit—the type of spoon you find in a tourist store full of inexpensive trinkets. We collect lots of ceramic, glass, and metal elephants. I collect salt and pepper shakers, some of which are quite kitschy. In Spain, I fell in love with Velasquez's masterpiece *Las Meninas*, which famously depicts the *Infanta* (young princess) Margaret Theresa and her entourage, including her *meninas*, or "ladies-in-waiting." During our travels, I started seeing miniature *meninas* everywhere, whether at a souvenir stand or a gallery. I began purchasing them, not realizing at the time what great table decorations they would make.

As modest as our events often were, they remained quite formal, which required some learning on our part. Ambassador school doesn't teach you which fork to use or how to conduct yourself at official affairs. Luckily, we already knew most of that. Equally important rules, however, dictate who sits where. At larger gatherings, the ambassador generally sits at the middle point of the table, with the spouse across from him or her. On either side of the ambassadorial couple sit the most important people among the invited guests. If you are seated to the right of the host or the hostess, you are a person of great consequence; the person seated to the immediate left is also significant.

Within the confines of these rules, Alan and I could add our own touches. For example, very rarely did we seat couples together. We wanted guests to meet new friends at our events and to feel included as part of the group, even if they were seated at the far end of the table. Sometimes we shook things up even more by putting the deputy chief of mission at the end of the table. Given his stature and importance, locating him at the end helped balance things out by lending everyone some prominence.

I paid a great deal of attention to protocol, respecting the rules and doing my best to represent the United States in a positive light. From my perspective, this was a "job," however unofficial, and I was taking it seriously. I was very proud to represent my country. But I did make a few *faux pas*, both as a hostess and as an invited guest.

One evening, at an elegant dinner party in our honor at the Italian ambassador's palatial home, I made a disparaging remark about the former Spanish dictator Francisco Franco. A hostile look passed over my dinner companion's face, and I quickly learned that I was seated next to a die-hard Franco supporter.

Oh no, I thought as he politely informed me that Franco did many positive things for the country. *I should never have said that!*

The rest of the dinner was civil, but I remained self-conscious. From then on, I was more careful, recognizing that it wasn't my place to comment on politics. People did know that we were President Obama's representatives, so I could safely support both democratic principles and Democrats with a capital *D*. I did, however, refrain from commenting on anything about the Spanish government or Spanish history that might prove controversial.

My other social breaches were comparatively minor. On some days, for instance, I went out to walk the dog and returned in my workout clothes to find an elegant official breakfast in progress. On such occasions, I would either sneak up the stairs so nobody saw me, or simply go in as I was and say hello. The latter wasn't a very Spanish way of conducting myself. Spanish women were always beautifully put together in public settings. But I didn't worry about it too much. Such awkward moments were inevitable in the ambassador's residence, which was both a private space for the ambassador and his family to live as well as a function hall where receptions, meetings, and other events took place. Most of the guests who came never ventured up the steps to our private rooms, and I made sure never to walk downstairs in my bathrobe. If some people saw me in my exercise clothes from time to time, I could live with that.

Given all the events we hosted, and my great interest in anything culinary, I'm proud to say that we never suffered a food disaster—although we did come close. On one occasion, we hosted a group of college students from Emory University who had come to Spain to study its Jewish history, retracing the historical migrations of Jews through southern Spain and then throughout Europe. Chef Gustavo said he would make pizzas for the event, but it turned out that he prepared only four small pies. As anyone with college-age children knows, that just won't do the job. The kids devoured those pizzas in just a few minutes, and we wound up sending Byron, one of our footmen, to buy more pies at the nearest pizzeria. As I am a Jewish mother, running out of food is simply not in my lexicon, no matter where in the world I happen to be.

As this last episode suggests, we hosted a variety of events for all different types of people. We held many gatherings in honor of visiting Americans and Spaniards. Some came for official business, and others were simply curious about the work we did.

We held some events for the embassy staff, including afternoon coffee events to which we would invite ten or fifteen embassy employees at a time. We scheduled this event every six weeks or so. It was nothing fancy: we sat together in our piano room and enjoyed cookies and light refreshments. We just wanted a chance to talk with embassy staff, hear their stories, and get to know one another. We'd ask the staff: "What brought you to the Embassy? What made you join the foreign service? What's something we might not know about you? What are some questions you have for us?" It was a wonderful way to get to know people and to help them feel valued. Even now, having been back home for a few years, I keep in touch with a lot of local Spanish staff whom I got to know through these coffee events.

We also invited members of the embassy staff to our formal events. Of course, with about 130 Foreign Service Officers (FSO) and another 240 or so Locally Employed Staff (LES) serving at the embassy, we couldn't include everyone at every event. But there was never a representational event—one hosted on the embassy's behalf—in which we didn't include at least some staff from all levels. Sometimes these invitations reflected the nature of the event itself. If we hosted an evening session related to military affairs, people from the military section might attend. If the event was culturally based, we invited people from the public diplomacy section. We always tried to include junior officers so they could get a feel for these events. This was a wonderful way to share the spotlight with staff, so not everything centered on the ambassador alone.

In addition to these events, Alan and I invited embassy staff to our private festivities on Thanksgiving and to our religious holidays such as Passover, Rosh Hashanah, and Hanukkah. We sought a way to share our heritage and values, both as Americans and as Jews, and I think staff members appreciated our efforts.

I also hosted a "girls' night" periodically, inviting a small group of women from the embassy over for *copitas*. We had a blast, laughing and carrying on like longtime girlfriends. *Girls' night* might not be the most politically correct term, but it worked for us. My only regret is that I didn't begin the tradition until our third year in Spain. Think of all the fun I missed out on during those first two years! These days when I go back to Spain, I reconnect with former girls' night regulars. We all go out for dinner and have a blast, just like old times.

※

JUST AS THE EMBASSY'S FORMAL social events were designed to facilitate diplomatic relations between the United States and Spain, our official duties included hosting government officials from the United States who came to Spain to conduct government business or to better understand our bilateral relationship. You often hear about folks in Congress making overseas trips, and you might wonder about the purpose of such trips—or if you're cynical, you might think these are just excuses to take a vacation. Yet our elected representatives take trips abroad for any number of important reasons.

Foremost among these is meeting with political leaders, government officials, and business leaders from other nations to understand the economic opportunities available for American companies. US leaders also try to build cultural ties between the United States and other nations. Some congressional delegations and government officials focusing on national security visit US military posts abroad. Alan often brought government officials to the south of Spain to the US naval base in Rota. In fact, one of Alan's major accomplishments during his tenure in Spain was negotiating an agreement with the Spanish government to locate four US-based navy destroyers in Rota.

My role varied when congressional delegations (known as CODELs) came to Madrid. During one CODEL, members' spouses and I visited a bilingual school, speaking to kids in several classrooms about our home states. I was paired with Gayle Wicker, wife of Senator Roger Wicker, a Republican representing Mississippi. Gayle told stories about growing up in Tupelo, Mississippi, famous for being Elvis's birthplace and also the inspiration behind Van Morrison's hit "Tupelo Honey." I talked about Massachusetts, the Red Sox, and Ted Kennedy, and the fact that Madrid and Boston are similar in many ways. Although Gayle and I differ in our political beliefs, we had a great time engaging with the children and with one another, forgetting all about party lines and voting records. The kids got to ask questions like, "What's your favorite food? What's the weather like? Who are your sports teams?" And then they asked us which Spanish *fútbol* team we rooted for.

It was impressive to see these youngsters speak English. They inspired me to become more proficient in Spanish. Without the benefits of youth, my attempts at language mastery were proving to be quite difficult indeed.

In addition to members of Congress, at times we hosted cabinet officials. Ray LaHood, who was US secretary of transportation at the time, took a few trips to Spain to explore the country's renowned high-speed rail system. Resembling bullets flying through the air, Spanish high-speed trains are sleek, well-organized, and exceptionally clean. Whether you purchase a business-class (*preferente*) seat or a less glamorous tourist-class seat, each section is tidy and comfortable. The trains run quietly and smoothly, allowing passengers to fall asleep, read a book, start a conversation, or enjoy some food in the dining car. Television monitors play movies that passengers can enjoy with complimentary headphones. Like on a transatlantic plane, each car posts how fast the train is going and how much time remains before the train will reach its destination.

During our adventures throughout the country, Alan and I have traveled on trains speeding at up to 180 miles per hour. I didn't really have a sense of how fast that is until the time Alan and I joined the Spanish secretary of transportation in the front car. Stepping into the small cabin, with its huge, impeccably clean glass windshield, we were surprised to find no engineer or conductor present in the front car with us. Everything was computerized.

As the train sped along, we got a rare frontward view of the tracks being progressively swallowed up by the train, faster than one wants to contemplate. The scenery whizzed by, and I fought off feelings of vertigo. Though it was dizzying, I remember thinking to myself, *Imagine how train travel like this could revolutionize transportation in the United States!* With such reliable mass transit in the northeast corridor, for example, we could travel from Boston to New York in little more than an hour, making life far easier for commuters and tourists alike. In Spain, it takes three hours to travel from Madrid to Valencia by car, but only ninety minutes by high-speed rail.

Perhaps most important and astonishing of all is that the trains run on time. Forget the adage about setting one's clock on Germany's train schedule; one could easily set it based on Spain's. The rail authority even offers a money-back guarantee if trains are late—which they never are.

On another occasion, we had the pleasure of hosting Secretary of State Hillary Clinton. Alan and I first got to know the Clintons during the early 1990s, when Bill Clinton was running for president. We saw them in many different places and contexts, including at Renaissance Weekend events held in Hilton Head, South Carolina. Renaissance Weekends are elite, invitation-only retreats where businesspeople and emerging leaders network and share ideas. Alan and I then hosted the Clintons numerous times during President Clinton's election cycles, and we worked for Hillary Clinton during her Senate campaign. In 2008, we decided to support Barack Obama for the presidency, but continued to hold Hillary in extremely high regard. I personally adore her and think of her as one of the smartest, most talented, and most capable people around.

In July 2011, when Secretary Clinton's plane landed at the Torrejón Air Base, Alan and I were there to greet her. Joining her motorcade, we went speeding into Madrid with front cars, tail cars, and police officers on motorcycles accompanying the delegation. Alan then accompanied the secretary as she met with her counterpart, Foreign

Affairs Minister Trinidad Jiménez, and with Prime Minister José Luis Rodríguez Zapatero. Later that day, they met with King Juan Carlos as well as with Mariano Rajoy, the leader of Spain's opposition party at the time.

When we arrived in Spain, Zapatero, the leader of the socialist party (the PSOE), was prime minister. As the economic recession worsened in Spain, Prime Minister Zapatero called for early elections, to be scheduled in the fall of 2011, and he stepped aside as his party's candidate in favor of Alfredo Pérez Rubalcaba. Part of Alan's job was to develop relationships with officials both in government and in the opposition, as relations with both parties would preserve America's position regardless of who was in power. Sure enough, during the 2011 election, the center-right party (the Partido Popular, or PP) swept into office with an absolute majority in the congress and parliament—and Rajoy was elected prime minister (a post he retained until 2018). In six hours of back-to-back meetings, Hillary Clinton met with all these leaders. Despite her grueling schedule, she took time to thank embassy staff during a meet-and-greet at the residence. Her graciousness, warmth, and professional demeanor were on full display. I so admire Hillary Clinton, and was so honored to host her in Madrid.

The many CODELs we hosted prepared us for Secretary Clinton and for Vice President Joe Biden, who visited in May 2010. The vice president was the highest-ranking American to visit Spain in over nine years. It was an honor to host him, and I'm happy to report that everything positive that people say about Joe Biden is true. He is a wonderfully nice man who takes time with you and focuses on you; he looks you in the eye and makes a connection. He kisses babies because he wants to, not because that's what politicians do.

Before Vice President Biden arrived, we made every effort to support and assist his advance team. His people made detailed arrangements for hotels and travel routes, vetting embassy staff who were scheduled to meet him. For weeks before his arrival, we held a daily, high-level, fifteen-minute standing meeting at the embassy to discuss all the moving parts associated with the visit. When Biden finally arrived, he traveled to a Spanish military base to visit soldiers who would soon be deployed to Afghanistan. A ceremony then followed on the base parade grounds, unfolding in accordance with strict military protocol. In his remarks at the ceremony, the vice president thanked the Spanish people and government for joining with the United States to help combat terrorism in Afghanistan, and to ensure that country would never again be a haven for the terrorists who plotted the attacks on 9/11.

Afterward, the embassy held an informal meet-and-greet, inviting all employees to attend. Biden thanked the staff for their service, spending time with every single person. That night, the vice president invited Alan and me to join him and his son Hunter for a small dinner with family and staff. Learning that Biden likes Italian food, we found an Italian restaurant in Madrid called Più di Prima and enjoyed a wonderful meal. Along with Biden's family, our party included the vice president's national security advisor, Tony Blinken, who later became deputy secretary of state, and his press spokesman, Jay Carney, who later became President Obama's press secretary. Being there, enjoying delicious Italian food after three straight months of Spanish food, we felt like part of the extended Biden "family." It was a wonderful way to get to know the vice president better.

☀

AS FUN AS JOE BIDEN'S visit was, we didn't need dignitaries in attendance to have a wonderful time at social events. In fact, included among the many events we attended and parties we hosted were some serious blowouts (if I do say so myself). First among these were our July Fourth celebrations.

Every embassy around the world celebrates its country's national holiday. France has its famous Bastille Day. Ireland has St. Patrick's Day. India, Germany, Japan, you name it—they all host annual events to celebrate their national heritage, inviting other ambassadors to attend along with locals and expats. Our Fourth of July events were beyond great—they were a highlight of my time in Spain.

The first year, we held our festivities on the front lawn, where over a dozen booths were set up and staffed by American food companies doing business in Spain. Vendors included Häagen-Dazs, Ben & Jerry's, Dunkin' Donuts, and Starbucks. Of course, Alan and I wanted to serve our favorite American foods: mini hot dogs and hamburgers, crab cakes, chicken wings, and all sorts of Independence Day favorites. A catering company provided the rest of the food as well as an assortment of beer (mostly Budweiser, of course), wine, and mixed drinks. With the booths lining the property's perimeter, the embassy grounds resembled a carnival. A live band played rock 'n' roll music, and people swayed to the rhythms on a dance floor erected just for this purpose.

While the size and scope of the festivities grew each year, that first celebration was especially memorable. Alan and I stood outside our residence in our driveway as all the guests approached us in a receiving line. We shook everyone's hand or exchanged the famous Spanish double kiss, and let the importance and genuineness of it all sink in deep. The guests, who numbered around two thousand, conveyed true pride in connecting to the United States through Alan and me. Back home, many Americans treat our Fourth of July celebrations more casually, maybe by going to a parade or attending a barbecue. In Spain, I found that our American independence celebrations took on real meaning—almost akin to religious celebrations. I got a sense that we truly were marking the birth of a country and a people, and I was pleased to see how much the Spanish admired our country and wanted to show their affection.

Adding significance to each of the four Independence Day celebrations we hosted was the formal presentation of the colors, performed by the embassy's marine detachment. The marines marched while carrying four flags, or "colors": the United States, Marine Corps, Spanish, and US State Department flags, all in holsters attached at their hips. They solemnly presented the colors to the ambassador, and a military band played both the American and the Spanish national anthems. The ceremony touched me to the core, especially as I placed my hand over my heart for the singing of "The Star-Spangled Banner." It was a different experience than, say, standing for the anthem at a ballpark. Here, everyone was facing in our direction—hundreds of people looked right at us, hands on their hearts, faces tinged with respect and love of our country. These moments were intimate, special—and unforgettable.

That first year, our two daughters stood on the platform alongside us as Alan made a speech welcoming everyone. In subsequent years, I contributed to the speeches, delivering each one in Spanish after practicing with my teacher, who would graciously spell the words out for me phonetically to help my pronunciation. While Alan focused his remarks on diplomatic relations between Spain and the United States, my comments were more personal, coming from the heart. I would talk about how welcome we felt in Spain, how proud we were to represent our country abroad, and how much meaning Alan derived from his work as ambassador.

Though each year was memorable and wonderful, 2012 was especially so because Spain had just emerged triumphant in the World Cup soccer tournament. I remember employing a particular Spanish term to describe the moment. Though used in a variety of settings, and roughly equivalent to the word *felicidades* (congratulations), the term *enhorabuena* was especially fitting that year because it literally means "a great hour." Indeed, it was. And as was the case every year, the party began after the speeches and continued until late in the night. We all had a total blast.

During the next three years of our tenure, the party grew too big for our front lawn. In 2011, Alan thought of holding the party at Madrid's City Hall, in Palacio de Cibeles—an early twentieth-century building designed in Gothic Revival style, originally serving as Madrid's central post office. Its iconic design, beautiful courtyard, and outlook towers offer excellent facilities for formal events. In its huge courtyard that year, embassy staff built a beautiful stage draped in red, white, and blue. Once again, vendors erected booths for traditional American food, a rock 'n' roll band played American favorites, and a large dance floor accommodated everyone who wanted to groove to the great music. In addition to being such a historic and picturesque location, Cibeles seemed to represent the merging of the American and Spanish traditions.

Not everyone at the embassy felt that way. Many preferred that the Fourth of July be celebrated on US soil—and legally, the embassy site is located on US territory. So in 2012 and 2013, the party moved back to the residence. But since we needed more space, we devised a plan to have the party both on the front grounds of the residence and in the embassy parking lot to the rear of the building. We had the parking lot covered in blue carpet, a stage set up with red, white, and blue bunting, and a US naval band performing old-time rock 'n' roll songs like "Johnny B. Goode" as well as songs by artists such as Van Morrison and Michael Jackson. While years 2010 and 2011 were successes, our final two Independence Day events raised the bar. They were truly magnificent.

At each of these celebrations, Alan and I were out in front, hitting the dance floor and firing up the party. Everyone wanted to dance with us. The staff danced heartily, and people just had a ball. Though we enjoyed all the events we hosted, the Fourth of July parties allowed us to let loose. We connected to the music, partied until the very last song was over, and drank copious amounts of wine and tons of gin and tonics. The guests' energy helped magnify and reinforce our own. Everyone invigorated one another as we shared an unselfconsciously joyful event.

By contrast, perhaps the most lavish social event we hosted was a black-tie Christmas party in 2012, honoring the American gold standard in jewelry, Tiffany & Co. Representatives of the company asked to meet with me, wanting to partner with us to boost their businesses in Madrid. As one of the embassy's roles is to support US businesses, this perfectly aligned with our mission. Everyone at the embassy (particularly those people involved with protocol) was very excited about this event. Such a high-profile party would mean an A-list group of guests.

Tiffany planned, paid for, and executed the holiday party along with a small team from the embassy. At the recommendation of Tiffany's event planner, the company lit the front of our residence in its signature robin's egg blue, with blue carpet lining the driveway. Tiffany also moved all the furniture out of our residence and lit every wall in a different color. Because the event was black-tie formal, a true gala, women arrived in long gowns and men in tuxedos. Along with the royal induction ceremony and the monarchy's annual diplomatic receptions, it marked one of three times I wore a long dress in Spain.

Greeting guests upon arrival were three Hanukkah menorahs and a ten-meter (thirty-foot) Christmas tree, surrounded by blue Tiffany boxes of all sizes. Tiffany hired entertainers to parade through the rooms on tall stilts, provided a model dressed as Audrey Hepburn from the film *Breakfast at Tiffany's*, and found the happiest Santa Claus ever.

The party went on and on. Shoes came off, a conga line formed, and we danced until the early morning hours.

※

WHILE I ENJOYED ENTERTAINING CODELS and attending fancy galas, from the start, I yearned for a deeper purpose and mourned the fact that "Susan the businesswoman" remained underutilized in Spain. Things began to change for me in March 2010 when I met Jaime Malet.

Jaime and I struck up a conversation at the Palacio de Cibeles, at a Madrid 2020 event to promote Madrid as a tourist destination. He serves as chair of the American Chamber of Commerce in Spain (AmCham Spain), an organization working to support American companies in Spain and Spanish companies in the United States. Through our conversation, Jaime learned that in the United States, I was a working woman who took pride in my career, and that I'd been involved with women through professional associations. He lit up at this news and suggested I work with his women's leadership committee at AmCham.

After several months in Spain, I was excited to chair the committee and become professionally involved. This opportunity seemed ideal: AmCham Spain partners directly with the US embassy, and I had experience and passion promoting women in business. Eager to begin, I invited all twenty members of the women's leadership committee to the embassy for a breakfast meeting. All twenty members showed up, which was highly unusual. Clearly, the US embassy was a draw.

The women on the committee occupied senior leadership positions in US companies like IBM, Pfizer, and Microsoft; top Spanish companies such as Indra, Banco Santander, and Grifols; and leading business schools like ESADE, IE, and IESE. With a translator assisting us in this meeting, we started to brainstorm together: What were the key issues facing the Spanish economy? How might we all address these issues from a woman's point of view?

These discussions led to a research project, spearheaded by the committee members who directed Spain's business schools. For this project, we interviewed twenty-four leading female business executives. Based on these interviews and additional research, we drafted and submitted to the Spanish government a comprehensive white paper about energizing the Spanish economy. Our findings were tangible and concrete, focusing on how to stimulate research and development opportunities and how to encourage entrepreneurship. The report was well received and thoughtfully considered, and some of its ideas were implemented.

As my involvement with Spanish women executives deepened, I began hosting roundtable listening sessions, where I tried to get a sense of the business landscape in Spain and the areas in which Spanish businesswomen needed support. After listening to women's experiences, the leadership committee and I identified another area of importance to women in business: the lack of opportunities for midcareer Spanish women to meet and learn from senior executives.

The committee joined forces, planning a series of events to address this problem. We invited CEOs to host eight to ten midcareer women for a discussion of how they arrived at the top as well as the challenges they faced along the way. Rafael Díaz-Granados, the president of General Electric (GE), Spain and Portugal, volunteered first. After that, Paloma Beamonte, CEO of Xerox Spain, hosted us. It was so interesting to connect with midlevel career women trying to move to the top, and it was inspiring to hear CEOs speak about surmounting career obstacles and other corporate challenges. To my surprise, Spanish and American women face strikingly similar workplace issues, not to mention similar struggles in maintaining work/life balance.

After further listening sessions about women's experiences, I also realized that Spanish businesswomen faced a severe lack of networking opportunities. While juggling all of their responsibilities in the corporate suite and at home, women have little time to talk with one another. Unlike men, women tend not to meet at the golf course or other traditional venues for informal networking. I wondered if I might gather Spanish and American women—including embassy staff and their families—to create a series of events that would fill this void. These events might draw attention to what Spanish women were doing, shining a light on their achievements as well as those of Spanish-based American companies. As an added benefit, it would also give embassy employees and families a chance to meet and network.

Such initiatives excited me because they paralleled my work with The Commonwealth Institute (TCI), an organization dedicated to helping businesswomen grow their organizations and realize their full potential. During my fifteen years serving on TCI's board, I helped support programs in Boston dedicated to female networking, mentoring, and general empowerment. For example, TCI organizes a series of important events, drawing luminaries like Senator Elizabeth Warren, Gloria Steinem, Speaker of the House Nancy Pelosi, and former secretaries of state Madeleine Albright and Condoleezza Rice.

TCI also runs a number of programs to help women business leaders thrive. Some of these include peer learning groups (called "circles") in which senior managers and female CEOs partner with CEOs, CFOs, or senior female executives in other companies. One of my favorite initiatives is called Strategies for Success (S4S), which brings midlevel career women together to explore issues relevant to their professions. Critical to S4S is pairing these women with TCI board members as mentors. While in Spain, I continued to serve as a midcareer mentor, talking to my mentee over Skype. I will confess that this was a two-way street: I learned as much from my mentee as she may have learned from me.

With these mentoring and networking events underway in Spain, even more ideas started percolating in my mind. I wondered how I could organize other embassy events to support women. These events wouldn't necessarily be affiliated with AmCham Spain, but they would align with the US embassy's existing priorities and initiatives.

As I considered various ideas and approaches, a tremendous and unforeseen opportunity arose. A friend of mine, Harvard Business School professor Rosabeth Moss Kanter, wrote to tell us of her upcoming business trip to Spain. Of course, Alan and I loved the idea that she was coming for a visit. While in Madrid, I asked her, might she be willing to do a breakfast event for us? We thought to convene Spanish and American businesswomen to discuss strategy and innovation in global business—precisely Rosabeth's research specialties.

Rosabeth graciously accepted. Working hard with the embassy's protocol and commercial services sections to develop a guest list, we anticipated forty to fifty attendees. In the end, however, over one hundred people attended. And Rosabeth was fantastic. A larger-than-life personality, she commands a microphone and speaks flawlessly, without notes. When she speaks about global competitiveness and what makes companies successful—topics on which she has written a series of books—people are instantly fascinated. After she addressed the crowd, most audience members stayed to spend extra time with her. We had a hard time getting people to leave! The entire dynamic simply clicked. You can't plan events like that—they are tremendous gifts that come your way, and you must enjoy them when they do.

Energized and inspired by Rosabeth's visit, I thought of potential subjects for future speakers and events. There was no shortage of good ideas. The real challenge for me was engaging embassy staff in the planning. Everyone at the embassy works hard and has plenty of work to do. In order for events to succeed, they had to fit in well with preexisting embassy initiatives. *Slowly but surely* became my mantra; I suggested further ideas for speakers, and embassy staff continued to turn me down, testing my patience. Despite these obstacles, I found an ally in Ellen Lenny-Pessagno, director of the embassy's commercial services department. A great supporter and advocate, Ellen was already committed to women's leadership, and we worked together to generate ideas that strongly aligned with strategic embassy objectives. With Rosabeth as the first solo speaker, we followed up with a whole series of events that I would later brand the "women's leadership series."

As these women's leadership events gained focus, visibility, and meaning, Ellen departed the embassy. I then began working with Nancy Brown, a fantastic American woman working in Spain, who also served as the global employment advisor for embassy families. She was deeply committed to networking and providing opportunities for local businesses to attract embassy family members seeking work in Spain. Together, we organized one event with Elvira Sanz, the female CEO of Pfizer, a leading American pharmaceutical company with a large Spanish presence. Following that, we hosted the leaders of the Spanish divisions of Facebook (Irene Cano), Hewlett Packard (Helena Herrera), Microsoft (Maria Garana), and Kindle (Coro Castellano)—all women.

Seeing the growing presence of women's leadership in the technology realm, I invited three female professionals to an event addressing the future of journalism. Lisa Abend is a Madrid-based American journalist who works for several publications, including *Time* magazine. Ana Romero is the foreign editor for one of Spain's largest daily newspapers, *El Mundo.* Lourdes Garzón is the executive director for Spain's edition of *Vanity Fair.* All three talked about changing technology, the death of print media, and the rise of online services. Each placed heavy emphasis on maintaining high quality at a time when readers are increasingly discerning. I was proud when over one hundred business leaders (mainly women) attended this event.

Still other speakers came from entirely different domains. I hosted a series of events on the topic of women and fashion, but I didn't want it to be simply about style and the latest trends. So I approached Covadonga O'Shea, head of a fashion business school in Spain; Cavan Mahony, who was in charge of Missoni (the high-end Italian fashion house) in Spain; and Tiziana Domínguez, who was taking over Adolfo Domínguez, her family's large chain of upscale clothing stores. These women spoke to over one hundred people about different aspects of women's fashion. After much initial planning, these events stood on their own, attracting many interested people.

Prior to becoming an ambassador's wife, I understood fashion events as social occasions instead of career-related, professional opportunities. Attending a Tiffany gala or a high-level fashion event was outside of my comfort zone and definitely not a typical activity of mine. From the outside looking in, such events appeared suited for "society ladies" instead of businesswomen like me. At the embassy, I learned that Spaniards don't typically distinguish between supposedly "social" events and professional ones. By hosting a glamorous event, Tiffany could expand its brand recognition. And by going to a fashion show, I could learn about a completely new business, make new business connections, and help further the embassy's strategic priorities.

One fashion premier I attended was especially fruitful. My host, Cavan Mahoney, mentioned that her stepfather was coming to Spain and encouraged me to do an event with him. As it turned out, he was none other than Professor Howard Stevenson, credited by *Forbes* with being Harvard Business School's "lion of entrepreneurship." When I broached the idea of Howard visiting, I initially feared some sensitivity on the part of the embassy. Promoting entrepreneurship was one of Alan's major strategic concerns. His economic team easily could have snatched this opportunity from me, insisting that their work took priority and that they needed to meet with Stevenson instead. To Alan's credit, however, he suggested that I host Howard for a women's leadership series. In early February 2012, Howard arrived in Spain. He lived up to his stellar reputation. I found him to be gracious, lovely, and accommodating, and his talk was terrific. Once again, we had managed to organize a great and productive event—thanks largely to serendipity, openness, and a bit of pushing.

One additional area I focused on, which was a key priority of Alan's as well, was philanthropy and volunteerism. At first blush, as I discovered before we founded Volunteers in Action, there didn't seem to be much volunteering in Spain. The country offers a strong safety net for its citizens, with the government, the church, and the family unit meeting many public needs, including health care, social services, and support for the arts. As economic times have changed, however, volunteerism has become more important among the Spanish people, and companies increasingly serve as patrons of museums and the arts.

The more we at the US embassy probed, the more we discovered a growing appetite for this type of service. So when the Spanish government and the European Union declared 2011 the Year of the Volunteer, we redoubled our efforts to support and encourage volunteerism and community service in Spain.

Having been involved for over thirty years in corporate social responsibility (CSR)—an extension of volunteerism—I have always believed that companies can be financially successful while at the same time serving as good corporate citizens. While at TPI, I helped shape and design philanthropy programs for corporations. I can attest to how gratifying it is to be part of the CSR community, and how such philanthropic efforts can bolster companies' success and mission. So in September 2011, I was thrilled to host a roundtable of leading Spanish philanthropists, including representatives from Telefónica, the largest telecommunications company in Spain, and Repsol, a global energy company.

With a team of translators in place, we discussed philanthropic initiatives in progress at each company and helped spur new ideas about corporate philanthropy in Spain. As I was fascinated to learn, Spanish corporations tend to channel their charitable efforts abroad, often venturing into the developing world. For example, a Spanish water company might fund improved water facilities and purification processes in South America, in the rural Andean countryside; infrastructure and construction companies might work on improving public works projects in India, Brazil, or developing regions in the Middle East or Africa. This contrasted with the American corporations I knew, which typically provide support to local charitable organizations, such as museums, hospitals, or universities.

I found the chance to host all these events extremely rewarding and enriching. I met amazing people and had some extraordinary, memorable experiences, which included joining a group of women to ring the opening stock exchange bell at the Spanish Stock Exchange building known as La Bolsa (which translates, appropriately, to "the pocketbook"). My work with AmCham Spain and the women's leadership initiatives represent a legacy of my time there. I'm proud to say that my efforts had some significant practical benefits. Thanks in part to these networking events, spouses, partners, and family members of embassy employees and military personnel were able to grow professionally and make important contacts—while others in the business world enjoyed the chance to gain new perspectives on entrepreneurship, responsibility, and leadership.

※

I WOULD BE REMISS IN writing a chapter about my official duties without mentioning a great side benefit: the opportunities I had to meet celebrities. I mingled with all kinds of famous actors, athletes, musicians, and other people, including Tom Cruise and Miss America 2011, Teresa Scanlon. Joan Baez, one of my musical "sheroes," came to receive the Order of Arts and Letters of Spain, bestowed by Spain's Ministry of Culture. Alan and I saw her in concert and greeted her after the award ceremony. When musical legend James Taylor came, we got a chance to spend time with him backstage. Warm and friendly, "Sweet Baby James" didn't disappoint. We had met him before, during the first Obama campaign, and during my WGBH days, I had worked with his wife Kim at the Boston Symphony Orchestra. It was great to see him again.

One of my favorite encounters was with another major luminary, Leonard Cohen. Alan and I have adored his music for decades, and we found him to be friendly, disarming, and quite gentle—very Zen-like. He came to Spain in 2011 to receive the prestigious Prince of Asturias Award for lifetime achievement for his poetry and novels, whose symbolism and blending of mystical and religious traditions have profoundly touched three generations. For this annual event, we traveled north to Asturias for the ceremony to celebrate and honor the American award recipients. Bestowed annually in the city of Oviedo, it is roughly the equivalent of a Spanish Nobel Prize. Many Americans—including Woody Allen, Arthur Miller, Bob Dylan, and Bill and Melinda Gates—have received the award. Though Cohen was technically a Canadian, he did live in Los Angeles, so we could claim him as "kind of American." Either way, Alan and I couldn't miss the opportunity to see him.

The night before the ceremony, the Jovellanos Theater in the nearby town of Gijón hosted a special tribute concert paying homage to

Cohen's versatility as an artist. An array of musicians, such as Javier Mas, the Webb Sisters, Glen Hansard, and Nacho Vegas, performed some of Cohen's most beloved songs, including "Dance Me to the End of Love" and, to honor his influence in Spain, "The Gypsy's Wife." Flamenco singer Juan Rafael Cortés Santiago, who uses the stage name Duquende, performed this masterful piece, which he typically plays alongside Cohen. The concert ended with a youth chorus singing "Hallelujah" in tribute to Cohen and his legacy.

Alan and I sat in a box right next to Cohen. After everyone had performed, he stood up, tipped his trademark fedora, and expressed his gratitude with a hand signal for *namaste*. It was just beautiful. Backstage, he sat and talked to everybody, including the kids, who swarmed all around him.

The niece of Spanish poet Federico García Lorca—one of Cohen's most important inspirations—received a special tribute in her uncle's honor when Cohen honored him in his remarkable speech at the Prince of Asturias awards ceremony. But perhaps the most poignant part of Cohen's remarks featured his unique connection to Spain. Four decades earlier, the audience learned, Cohen had acquired a beautifully executed Conde guitar fashioned from cedar wood. He described how, the previous night, he had removed the instrument from its case and beheld the still fragrant, living wood. He recounted that an inner voice had said to him, "You're an old man, and you have not said thank you. You have not brought your gratitude back to the soil from which this fragrance arose." And so that's why Cohen had come to Spain, to thank "the soil and the soul of this people" who had given him so much, including the guitar that had helped translate his poetry into music.[1]

---

1   "Leonard Cohen: The Prince Of Asturias Awards Speech With Annotations & Commentary," Cohencentric: Leonard Cohen Considered, https://cohencentric.com/leonard-cohen-the-prince-of-asturias-awards-speech-with-annotations-commentary.

During the awards ceremony, Alan sat on the stage along with the Spanish prince and princess, the award recipients, and the ambassadors of other countries whose citizens received awards. I sat in a box that faced Queen Sofia. When we left the theater, the streets of Oviedo were lined with people dressed in Asturian costumes and playing *gaitas* (traditional Spanish bagpipes) and other traditional instruments. Everyone cheered as the awards ceremony attendees paraded through town and back to the hotel for a celebratory reception.

Of the many celebrities we met, another favorite who made a huge impression on me was tennis star Rafael Nadal. He came to the embassy needing to renew his US visa. Knowing what a national hero he was, Alan invited him over to meet some of the embassy's Spanish staff. We gathered a group of twenty Spanish employees, all of whom were over-the-top excited to meet Rafa. He talked to every single person—signing the tennis balls we had bought bearing the Roland-Garros logo of the French Open, where he has dominated men's tennis—and took photographs with anyone who wanted one.

Rafa came with his small entourage: his trainer, his coach at the time (who is also his uncle), and his best friends. Dressed in a crisply pressed blue shirt with jeans that fit him perfectly, Rafa is exceptionally handsome, in exquisite shape, and unbelievably gentle in spirit. We talked for a few minutes, and I asked him how he was doing, what it was like to be on the road, and if it was true that he was such an ardent Real Madrid fan. His English was excellent.

When it was time to say our goodbyes, Alan and I presented Rafa with an American flag, folded in a box, that was flown in his honor outside the embassy that day. We took pictures together, and I posted one on my Facebook page. It received ninety-eight "likes" within minutes, which I thought was pretty exciting. When Rafa put the same photo on his Facebook page with the comment "Thank you to my friends at the US embassy," he got 29,000 "likes"—quite the fan club.

That night, Alan and I went to the Real Madrid game, and sitting a few rows in front of us was Rafa. He came over to say hello and to thank us again. He may be one of the world's greatest tennis players, but we found him as down to earth as could be. It was incredibly special to spend time with such a gentleman.

※

WHEN I FIRST ARRIVED IN Spain, I perceived the role of hostess as somewhat frivolous. In the end, it became something I truly enjoyed and valued. Our social events exposed us to different layers of Spanish society. During our parties and get-togethers, we learned about the lives of Spaniards and the politics of Spain, and we helped expose Spanish people to American society and values. I felt grateful to be giving back in some small way, whether by helping businesswomen make contacts and build their careers, or by supporting Alan's important diplomatic initiatives. Almost all our events had meaning and purpose to them, and accomplished concrete objectives.

Through my hosting activities, I learned that the role of the ambassador's spouse carried weight, and that this weight or power extended outside the embassy. I would write to people whom I never would've dreamed of contacting before, and they would actually answer me! I once invited Elena Arzak, a top woman chef in Spain, to talk about food. A leading gastronomy publication had just named her Basque restaurant, Arzak, number one in the world. She replied by saying how much she'd like to participate but she had a conflict, which she greatly regretted. The president of Google Spain, Javier Rodriguez Zapatero, accepted my invitation to come speak, as did the leaders of many companies, institutions, and organizations. As I planned these events, I realized my power to get things done. I learned that I could reach out and partner with others, uniting people in enriching ways.

We brought people together in fun ways, too. And I'm not just talking about the Wienermobile. At Easter time, we'd invite all the embassy children for an Easter egg hunt and pictures with the Easter bunny. In Madrid, Easter was always a sunny day with temperatures in the seventies (or twenties, in Celsius). Plastic eggs filled with chocolate were scattered all over the lawn, and the young boys and girls arrived in their Easter finest. The Easter bunny would always emerge from our residence door and come hopping along. Everyone wanted his or her picture taken with the furry creature, and Alan was more than happy to accommodate them by dressing in costume.

On one occasion, a three-year-old boy attended the Easter egg hunt in April, and later returned in December for our Christmas celebration. On Santa's lap, he leaned over to his mother and said, "I can't believe Santa Claus lives here. It's the same house as the Easter bunny." It was just too sweet. Although most of the events we hosted had a serious purpose, these light-hearted events were often—in their own ways—just as rewarding.

SEVEN

FROM THE MOUNTAINS OF MADRID TO THE COAST OF BARCELONA

W ITH LESS THAN FOUR YEARS for our tour in Spain, Alan and I anticipated that intimate friendships and close connections would be in short supply. Ambassador school confirmed this. As one instructor warned, "You're not going to make friends easily. It's just not going to happen. You're the ambassador. Nobody even calls you by your first name." Of course, I knew that Spain would be a life-changing experience, and I wanted to embrace it eagerly. But it was hard to leave my home and social network in Boston. I was not good at saying goodbye to regular walks with friends and their puppies, opportunities for impromptu lunches with my daughters, and of course, easygoing conversations of all kinds—in English. Our cherished friends and family would be deeply missed.

In mid-February 2009, we celebrated Alan's sixtieth birthday with Joan and Steve, two of our dearest friends. They knew that Alan had been asked to be an ambassador, and that at some point in the year we would move abroad, but they didn't yet know which country it would be. For the occasion, we went to Twin Farms, a small, intimate resort in southeast Vermont—one of our favorite places in the world. We knew life was about to throw us a curveball, so it was a trip tinged with bittersweet emotion.

Nestled in three hundred acres of forest, Twin Farms has served for two decades as a special sanctuary and refuge for the four of us. We go there to unwind, rejuvenate, and connect, staying in one of the freestanding, exquisitely appointed, thematically designed cottages: one looks like an old barn, one sits amid an apple orchard, others resemble Tuscan and Moroccan bungalows. No matter the theme, each cottage is adorned with beautiful artwork and furnishings. During each visit, we notice something new. In this bucolic paradise, we've never needed sunny days or scheduled activities. We simply arrive and open ourselves up, allowing our senses to be aroused and a deep state of relaxation to set in.

Over the years, we've become acquainted with the staff at Twin Farms—some are even Dead Heads like me. We especially look forward to seeing the amazing chef, Nathan, who has a particular talent for serving what each diner loves and avoiding what he or she hates. Raw onions have never appealed to me, and I have never seen one on any dish placed in front of me here. But the best part is the sumptuous surprises. If you crave a burger, you'll never receive a standard one. Rather, you might get specialty burgers the size of your thumb, complete with exotic mushrooms and freshly foraged greens from the Vermont countryside.

For Alan's birthday, he and I stayed high in the trees in the glass-framed Aviary suite. This cottage has beautiful stone glass décor, floor-to-ceiling windows, and rich leather and wood trimmings. As Joan and Steve were sitting with us in this gorgeous setting, Alan and I announced that we had something important to say. We had given some thought to how we would like to tell them, and we decided it would involve music.

Bob Dylan's "Boots of Spanish Leather" fit the bill: a song about leaving for a land across the ocean. Upon hearing Dylan's famous line about the mountains of Madrid and the coast of Barcelona, Joan and Steve turned to us and in unison exclaimed, "You're going to Spain!"

All four of us burst into tears—of joy, certainly, but also sadness at the prospect of our impending separation. This announcement made the trip even more real. We understood that our departure for Spain would represent a loss, that we wouldn't have the same familiar closeness we were used to. During our times together, Joan, Steve, Alan, and I don't simply discuss the weather or trade our most recent news. We discuss difficult issues like the need for more balance and kindness in our lives, and challenging moments we experience within our families. We all feel very blessed to have this rare type of authentic friendship, and I was already wondering how I would manage to leave it behind when we departed for Madrid.

Months later, when Alan and I were in ambassador school, I had a free day and decided to take myself to the movies. The future ambassadors were being flown to a secure military location to meet with senior leaders in the Department of Defense, where they would receive high-level briefings in national defense, military operations, and homeland security. I chose a noon showing of *It's Complicated* and walked into the theater, only to find I was the only person there. I changed my seat a number of times, and as the lights dimmed, I recognized a metaphor in my situation: I could have any seat in the house I wanted, but I was alone. I had yet to realize how complicated my life would become.

Was this the way I would feel in Spain? I was about to participate in all these amazing adventures, and experience all sorts of new things—but would I feel utterly alone?

Spain did turn out to be a difficult adjustment socially. But as time passed, the frequent visits from our dearest friends and family, as well as acquaintances and curious outsiders, nourished my soul. I managed to make meaningful social connections in Spain, learning to relate in unexpected ways. Whether through the synagogue, the women's leadership events, or my walks with Stella through the streets of Madrid, I met people unexpectedly and developed lasting bonds. Through the process of learning the Spanish language, I forged friendships and absorbed a greater understanding of Spanish customs and culture. Thanks to the transatlantic exchange of people—and letters, in the form of my Holas—I was even able to maintain and strengthen older friendships while also creating new ones.

All of this allowed me to grow as a person while in Spain and, eventually, to develop a reassuring sense of rootedness.

❦

IN SEPTEMBER 2009, AS ALAN and I prepared to leave for Spain—unaware that his nomination would be put on hold in the Senate—our house was in chaos. Teams of moving men were everywhere, putting our clothing into wardrobes and arranging the tchotchkes we had chosen to bring with us. Luckily, we weren't selling our house or moving everything out. We were fortunate to find a wonderful woman, Nancy, who would live in our house and keep watch over it. She and I coordinated logistics so that she would feel at home in the house but also know all its intricacies. The three days to pack our house into boxes and trucks were really a gift, distracting me from thoughts about leaving our friends and our broader social network.

While stressful for Alan, the delayed nomination was yet another gift to me, providing me more time to savor friendships. I took every opportunity to cherish my remaining time in Boston and to bond with my friends.

Alan and I shared the Jewish High Holidays with my sister Beth and her family, following our personal tradition: each of us prepares a special dinner on one of the two holiday nights. That year, Alan and I hosted the first night, inviting our daughters, my parents, Beth and Jeff, and their three daughters, Amy, Debbie, and Amanda. On the second night, we went to Beth's house. A wonderful cook, Beth started the festivities with Spanish foods—Marcona almonds, *tortilla española*, manchego cheese, and flavorful Spanish wines. It was so sweet and thoughtful of her, though it came with a sting. Everyone was excited for us, but also sad that we'd be leaving.

Around the same time, Ronni and Alice—two of my closest friends—organized a small goodbye party for me. I asked each of the thirteen invited guests for a framed photograph of herself that I could place on my desk or my bookshelves in Spain. Each guest also wrote something special for me in a card—such beautiful sentiments that I still become teary just thinking about it. I sat there with tears streaming down my face as people expressed how much they'd miss me. I knew I'd dearly miss them as well.

I had wanted to give all these friends something special. A book I had recently heard about on an NPR interview—*The Girls from Ames*, by Jeffrey Zaslow—seemed to be the perfect choice. It chronicled the lives of a group of childhood female friends in Ames, Iowa, depicting the beauty of friendship as these women navigated sickness, marriage, divorce, child rearing, and other life milestones. I also gave everyone a CD with some of my favorite music: songs like Jackson Browne's "Take It Easy," the Grateful Dead's "Uncle John's Band," and Phil Ochs's "Changes." Meaningful and melancholy, all these pieces contained rich statements on friendship, love, and loss.

When we arrived in Spain three months later, I was again distracted, this time by the steep learning curve attached to becoming an ambassador's wife. As a naturally outgoing person, I had assumed that I would hit the ground running and make new friendships to fill the gap created by the ones I was leaving behind in Boston. Unfortunately, this was not the case. I would soon become keenly aware of how socially isolated Alan and I were.

Arnold Chacon and his wife, Alida, hosted a luncheon to help orient me to my new role. Alida invited about twenty people from the embassy, selecting individuals with whom I would have to interface. Among the group was Dr. Peralba, a physician informally known as Dr. P. I didn't realize I'd be interacting with the health unit, but Alida did, and she made sure Dr. P and I were introduced. Also there was Angelines, who served as head of the legal section in the consular department. An embassy veteran, Angelines began work in the early 1960s when she was a student. She told the very moving story about how during this time—in the Franco era—the US embassy was the only place where she could participate in free and open conversations about the world. Sarah Genton, the community liaison officer, was there too, along with Mickey Robinson, a woman who headed the Navy Exchange. The Madrid Embassy had a small Navy Exchange, the NEX, located in the basement of the embassy building at the time. I was curious to hear everybody's story and make personal connections. Yet although these men and women were simply lovely, I quickly realized that while we might like one another, the embassy staff couldn't help but observe a strict formality with me. Because of my role as "the ambassador's wife," we could be colleagues—but it would be much harder to become friends.

It was also hard to become friends with diplomats from other countries. But I tried, and I'm glad I did. Within weeks of our arrival, the Japanese ambassador hosted an evening for all the G7 countries—Germany, France, Japan, Canada, the United States, Great Britain, and Italy. There, I learned that most ambassadors to Spain live on the outskirts of Madrid, in a suburb called Puerta de Hierro. Alan and I drove to this community, and instead of entering a hybrid work/residential arrangement like the US embassy, we entered a gracious, elegant, suburban home. The menu, which featured cuisine described as Spanish-Japanese fusion, was quite a treat. We began with prawn rolls with lotus rhizome, vegetables and mushrooms with sesame "salsa," crab-fried anchovies, and California-style maki rolls. We then had sea bass, tuna, and beef sashimi, steamed *huevos revueltos* with truffles, and grilled lamb with soy and ginger salsa.

After the meal, the fourteen attendees broke into two groups, 1950s-style—the men going into one part of the living room, the women into another. This was quite a surprise for someone accustomed to the mingling of the two sexes. Aside from the Japanese and German ambassadors' wives, everyone spoke English. As we conversed, I discovered that these were really nice women. They were, furthermore, all friends, forming part of a book group, going on walks together, and residing together in the same neighborhood. I left on an optimistic note, thinking that developing friendships in Spain might be a possibility.

When I mentioned this in an email to several of the spouses I had met during ambassador school, however, one woman quickly responded that these weren't the friends I should seek. "You want to be friends with Spanish people," she advised.

That advice took the wind out of my sails, and I wasn't sure I agreed with it. I really wanted to connect with people. What did it matter whose wives they were?

After the dinner party at the home of the Japanese ambassador, I reconnected with these women through the Asociación de Damas Diplomáticas, an organization that later changed its name to be more inclusive of male and female spouses. I went to several meetings, all conducted in Spanish. One was held in the old La Latina barrio of Madrid in an Italian cultural center that had recently been refurbished.

The place was done up in Missoni fabrics: a vivid swirl of signature Missoni purples, pinks, and reds. My mind was as turbulent as this amazing décor; I had trouble understanding the Spanish, and I felt lost.

There were still other opportunities for social engagement. Many of the ambassadors' wives, I learned, took a course on Spanish history together at the local Complutense University of Madrid. I thought this was a marvelous idea. What better way to learn history and culture while at the same time bonding with new friends? Alida offered me a ride to the Complutense, where I attended a class with them. Fearing that I would not understand a class conducted in rapid Spanish, I asked Virginia Ghent, a translator from the embassy, to accompany me. But her "whisper translation" (a term for providing English paraphrases of the professor's words in hushed tones) was far from the wonderful experience of Antonio Banderas whispering explanations during the Holy Week festivities in Málaga. I found it distracting in a university context, and so did my fellow students. So I scratched this class off my list of things to do while in Madrid.

Perhaps if I had lived in the suburbs near those ambassadors' wives, we would have become closer friends. Other opportunities to make friends existed, but I found myself similarly hamstrung. I was constantly invited to social events, but often I was so busy traveling with Alan or attending to embassy business that I couldn't follow up. My schedule was erratic. I couldn't easily pull someone aside and declare, "Every Tuesday morning, let's take a walk with our dogs." And although all sorts of Spanish clubs existed to welcome and integrate foreigners—including the American Women's Club and the International Newcomers Club—I just didn't have the time to attend events with any regularity.

I resigned myself to the reality that making friends wasn't going to come easy. There were just too many obstacles preventing relationships from forming—my own self included.

At times, I could be my own worst obstacle. Feeling the need to keep my guard up didn't help. Constantly aware of my public role and associated responsibilities, I was careful not to complain or utter my true feelings too often. Even though I kept asking people to call me Susan rather than Mrs. Solomont or "the ambassador's wife," I was self-conscious. The culture at the embassy was hierarchical. I knew people were observing me, and I wanted to make sure I did things correctly—though I didn't yet know what "correctly" meant.

When I was approached to join the American Women's Club, I was asked to serve as honorary chair. This awareness that I would be performing an important role set me on edge; I couldn't just be myself, which was what I really longed for. Trying to figure out where I fit in and what was expected of me didn't help me shed my self-consciousness. And I would need to shed it if I were to approach people in anything approximating a genuine way.

All of this meant that in the beginning, I was lonely. I missed having friends. And I missed the independence that I was used to in Boston—a personal and professional life independent of Alan and his job. For months on end, I was at a loss about how to solve this predicament.

※

A STEADY STREAM OF VISITORS from home filled the void somewhat. From close friends and family to casual acquaintances to friends of friends of friends, lots of visitors ventured to Spain to spend time with us. People seemed to come out of the woodwork, telling us they were headed to Madrid and expressing how much they'd love to stay with us. We hosted almost everyone who asked, usually saying no only when our schedules didn't permit or for one of our frequent absences from the embassy on trips.

On one occasion, the grandson of my cousin's best friend's next-door neighbor's relatives from California (I'm not exaggerating!) was traveling on a teen tour, and we hosted his group of teenagers. I decided that the tour had to have meaning—and in this case, it was an occasion to explain to late adolescents what an embassy is and how it functions. Fifty young teens filed into our dining room at three in the afternoon and fidgeted about as I gave a PowerPoint presentation, just as you would expect thirteen- or fourteen-year-olds to do. I served soft drinks and cookies, which they devoured, and then facilitated a question-and-answer session. I enjoyed debunking myths and sharing the important role of diplomacy with young, growing minds.

People often wondered why I extended myself like this, taking valuable time from embassy responsibilities to entertain people I barely knew. I felt it was part of our role to demystify what an embassy and ambassadorship were all about. I can't say whether it was a good use of my time—such things are impossible to quantify—but it was fun, and I can say that I'm glad I did it.

When I hosted the students from Emory University—that time we ran out of pizza—the connection was made through one of my doctors in the United States, whose daughter was part of that group. My daughter Stephanie had told me she knew one of the boys coming—she had met him once at a youth dance years earlier, where they had kissed in the coat closet—but she couldn't remember his name. When the kids were all gathered together at the embassy, I announced that I had some kind of relationship with three of them: "One of you is my doctor's daughter. Would you wave your hand?"

The doctor's daughter waved.

"One of you is the niece of my sister-in-law Debra, who lives in Israel. Would you raise your hand?"

My sister-in-law's niece waved.

"The third one knows my daughter Stephanie—and you know what went on with her in the coat closet at Temple Beth Elohim. So I won't embarrass you."

He turned crimson, and I moved quickly on. It was a funny moment, but on a serious level, I really wanted to spend time with these kids and support them in their cultural learning.

Almost all of our closest friends from America came to visit, eager to understand what our life was like and to spend time with us. They also wanted to see Spain, and to discover the riches of Madrid in particular. I learned early on that when friends visited, I had to arrange activities to occupy them.

Marci, one of my dearest friends, visited within two weeks of our own arrival. Always full of energy, she was up for anything and wanted to visit all the major tourist destinations; go on long, rambling city walks; and discover everything Madrid had to offer. I was still somewhat in a fog, overwhelmed by this new place and my new role. I felt as though I was being pulled in too many directions—by meetings at the embassy and a friend who wanted to experience everything with me by her side. Then, only several days into her planned trip, Marci revealed that she felt she was in the way. "This has been wonderful," she said, "but I think it's time for me to leave."

It was hard for me to see her go, because I love her dearly, and I knew it was disappointing for us both. Years later, we still talk about this difficult experience—a case of bad timing. Luckily, Marci and I have one of those friendships that doesn't skip a beat, even when difficulties arise. I'm happy to say that we remain dear friends to this day.

As time went on and I learned more about our adopted home, I began to take on the role of travel agent for our visitors. Yet I also had responsibilities and goals of my own to fulfill in Spain. I'm not a person who is good at saying no, but I learned that sometimes you have to do just that.

Plus, for me, there are only so many times you can tour the Royal Palace or view the ten most popular paintings in the Prado Museum. So, to streamline the process, I created some visitor's guides to the city.

My guide booklets, highlighting Madrid's major attractions, enabled visitors to strike off on their own and allowed me to do my own work. But there were a few things my guests and I would always do together. For example, we would always have one embassy dinner served either in the piano room (for a small foursome) or in our formal dining room (for a larger group). We dined using elegant State Department china, serving our own fine wines, and savoring Gustavo's (or Rosita's) excellent cooking. If guests were around for more than one night, we would also go out for dinner at one of our favorite Madrid restaurants.

Sometimes, guests would accompany us on official outings. Friends came to watch Alan give speeches, host roundtables, and anchor events such as the Global Youth Conference, a leadership program for high school students modeled on the United Nations. My girlfriends Ronni and Nancy came to visit during one of my first women's leadership events, watching as I interviewed my featured guest that week. My dear friend Alice visited a number of times, gaining new insights into Embassy life with each trip. You'd know she had visited because Stella would have bright red lipstick marks all over her face from being showered with Alice's kisses. Cindy and Sharyn came to visit as well and were perfect guests, finding their way around Madrid on their own and seeing all the great sights. Our visitors' excitement and enthusiasm about our life was palpable. Alan recalls going to a gallery opening with our dear friend Elliot, who was in town for a visit. Elliot was shocked that paparazzi outside were shooting Alan's photo—that a guy he went to college with was being treated like a celebrity.

Our guests really appreciated the many small benefits that came with being the ambassador's friend. When my girlfriend Nancy came with her husband, Mark, we traveled to San Sebastián, a beautiful coastal city in the northern Basque region, to see a Bruce Springsteen concert. It turns out that the Boss loves Spain as much as we do: for that leg of his tour, he played six nights in five Spanish cities. Our driver escorted our entire party to the gate of the concert venue—no long lines to suffer through. That night saw a torrential rainfall, and while we enjoyed the concert from covered seats, the other fifty-five thousand concertgoers got soaked. Even Springsteen got caught in the deluge. In true Bruce spirit, he opened his show with a version of Creedence Clearwater Revival's classic "Who'll Stop the Rain."

Alan and I generally had little hassle with tickets to shows, events, or museums, nor did we have to think about parking or making dinner reservations. When we visited the Prado, for instance, we were deposited right at the front door, circumventing the long lines of eager tourists and art-loving city dwellers. In San Sebastián—home to more Michelin-starred restaurants than any other place on earth—we topped off the Springsteen concert with a visit to three-starred Akelarre. As our friends often told us, they felt as though they were stepping into a magical world.

Frankly, so did we.

※

PERHAPS MY MOST BELOVED TRADITION with guests was a pastime that lacked any glamour whatsoever. Every friend visiting the embassy, bar none, asked to accompany me on a walk with Stella. This gave us the chance to talk about life and catch up. Our conversations went deep, touching on difficult feelings like my pangs of homesickness. Thanks to this tradition, I reestablished some sense of connection with my old life in Boston. Unfortunately, I always felt bereft when our guests left.

Some visits were especially memorable. As Alan and his dear friend Chester engaged in business ventures together over the years, I also became close friends with his wife, and we got to know their six children, those children's spouses, and their brood of around twenty grandchildren. Diane was the one who, when she and Chester visited, decided to teach Gustavo how to make challah. We assembled all the ingredients to bake two challah loaves, one in three braids and another in six, both covered in an egg glaze. Now, Gustavo didn't speak much English, and Diane and I spoke only broken Spanglish. Cristina did her best at narration, and we all laughed together as Diane taught everyone how to braid the bread. Sharing that moment in the kitchen added a whole new dimension to my relationship with Diane. For many months afterward, Gustavo baked challah for us on Friday nights, and I would reminisce about Diane and Chester's visit.

Our longtime friends Jerry and Leah—along with their grown kids, Ben and Caroline—also shared a memorable visit with us. Each day, we would take a long walk past the Columbian embassy, a reminder that Ben and Caroline had been adopted as young babies from Colombia. We couldn't have planned something that special and intimate—it just happened.

During their visit, I was eager for Leah to see what my life was like, so I invited her and Caroline to join us for a small luncheon with three other Spanish women. As these Spanish women were longtime friends, they focused only on one another and barely stopped talking the entire time. Poor Leah and Caroline could hardly get a word in. You would think that at some point, the Spanish women would have reached out to my guests and tried to get to know them. Not at all! They proceeded as if my visitors weren't even present. It wasn't rude per se—just a different way of conducting a social situation. As Leah commented to me afterward, my role was not easy, but certainly amusing.

To this day, Alan and I still laugh about the funny experience when our friends Geoff and Amy came to visit. As the friends who first introduced Alan and me at their Super Bowl party, Geoff and Amy have an enormous place in our hearts. During their visit, we were all invited to a dinner party at the home of an important businessman, the chairman and CEO of a global energy company. As always, we received in advance the protocol team's list of who would be there. One woman on the list was the minister of defense, a high-ranking official in the Spanish government. I prepped Amy about where this official lived, her family, and so on—just enough information to strike up a conversation—and I explained how unusual it was for a woman to preside over Spain's defense ministry. When we were seated for cocktails, Amy and I found ourselves flanking the minister on both sides. We peppered her with questions: "How do you find working in the ministry? How old is your son? How do you juggle all these important tasks?" She just gave us a blank stare.

We asked about her work in the government. She seemed to have no idea what we were talking about.

We then asked about her dog. Again—blank stare.

I figured that Amy and I weren't using our language skills very well—until we finally discovered that the minister had to cancel that evening, and that this woman shared her name but was a different person entirely. Wrong woman, wrong questions. No wonder she looked at us strangely!

Amy and I remember this fondly, thinking what fools we made of ourselves. I don't think our dinner companion was offended, but we felt silly for having been so completely misinformed.

Far from being whimsical, other visits were more eye-opening. My former TPI boss, mentor, and personal hero Peter Karoff came to visit with his wife, Marty. While they were in Madrid, they spent their days off on their own, going to museums and soaking up the rich cultural life. Marty, however, was in a wheelchair, and during her stay, we realized how inaccessible the residence was. While we did have an elevator, there were no other measures in place to accommodate Marty. The embassy didn't have funds dedicated for home improvements, but facilities management creatively found a way to make the residence more wheelchair accessible. After all, this was the US embassy, and we were not in compliance with the Americans with Disabilities Act (ADA). Shame on us, but kudos to the Karoffs for helping us rectify the problem.

As much of a blessing as it was to have friends around, the sheer volume of visitors could often feel burdensome. Sometimes, I received multiple emails from eager visitors and shuddered at the thought of their arrival. How would I host them with all of my responsibilities at the embassy? Alan couldn't understand my misgivings. He didn't appreciate that the responsibility of hosting fell entirely to me, nor did he understand my need for some privacy. I felt lonely much of the time, he reasoned, so why wouldn't I want friends to visit? And yet sometimes, I didn't. I just wanted to get on with my life in Spain and enjoy a bit of solitude.

When friends weren't visiting, we received visits from family members—like the time we celebrated my sister Beth's sixtieth birthday at the world-famous El Bulli, in the town of Roses, located along Cataluña's picturesque Costa Brava. We sampled every food, consumed several bottles of wine, and laughed endlessly. What a great memory!

I was especially happy to receive my mother, who visited after my father had passed away. Coming to Spain was a big deal for her. Though she and my father were once world travelers, their time abroad had dwindled once he became sick. When she arrived, we gave her the royal treatment. Everyone closely attended to her: "Mrs. Lewis, can we get you this? Can we help you in any way?"

On one occasion Adelina ironed my mother's nightgown so meticulously that the tiny ruffles on the yoke came out perfect. My mother was blown away—and she hasn't worn that nightgown to this day! "How can I wear it?" she says. "It would never look so perfect again."

The entire household fell in love with my mom, and in the end, they gave her a parting gift: beautiful Spanish towels with scenes of matadors and bullfighting. We had shown her Alan's office, attended official events with her, and taken a day trip to the beautiful art town of Cuenca. Though my mother had slowed down a bit and couldn't do too much walking, she really did get a sense of our life in Spain.

Alan's family visits presented different challenges because his brothers and their families are observant Jews who eat only kosher foods. We had to find the right foods for them and make sure we were attending to them correctly and respectfully. In Spain, even if you order something vegetarian in a restaurant, you still might get a dish with cured ham or pork in it. You can never be sure whether non-kosher beef, chicken broth, pork product, or shellfish might have been used in the food preparation. I was therefore especially grateful that the residence's kitchen staff rose to the occasion, ensuring that all the foods they prepared were in line with Jewish dietary laws.

Alan's youngest brother, Ahron (whom we call Max); his wife, Sheera; and their three children, Joseph, Aleeza, and Yakira came to visit with the goal of soaking in the Spanish culture. They wanted to see everything in Madrid, and then they took a day trip to Toledo. They were very independent, but we found time to swim in the residence's pool with the kids. When Alan's brother Jay and his wife, Debra, came from Israel with their youngest son, Eitan, they brought cans of kosher food and sought out a synagogue to observe daily prayers. They, too, soaked up everything and had a wonderful time. Finally, Alan's brother David and his wife, Joan, visited with their youngest daughter, Lauren.

They had an amazing experience, seeing Alan give speeches and riding in the official vehicle with us. The whole family really wanted to understand this experience. Our time together was special, and I think it deepened our relationships with all of them.

In the case of family and friends who didn't visit in person, I stayed connected through my group emails—my Holas. Upon arriving in Spain, I was flooded with emails from people asking me how I was and what I was up to, and I found myself writing the exact same thing to everyone. As with my travel guides, I decided to simplify the process. Even though my Holas were addressed to many people—who could have guessed how quickly the recipient list would swell to three thousand!—I thought of them as private communications. My thirty-four Holas started out as intimate accounts of the joys I was feeling and the sadness I experienced from time to time. As the readership grew, they became less personal and more informative. My early Holas discussed our residence in great detail, but I was told that this could compromise security. Afterward, I made sure to stay within bounds.

Sometimes I still ran into trouble. While visiting Spain, Ariana Huffington got wind of my Holas and asked to publish them in the *Huffington Post*. I was thrilled, but felt some trepidation about exposing myself to a larger audience. As it turned out, the State Department had other concerns. After seeing my online posts, government officials asked me to promptly remove them. It ticked me off that the State Department—which, up to that point, had expressed zero interest in my activities—suddenly objected to my decision to share some of my experiences. But I complied, and felt some relief at rediscovering my privacy.

Even years after our return, the Holas still resonate. Not long ago, someone emailed me asking about how to read them to prepare for leading a group to Spain in the springtime. I passed them along so the person could get acquainted with the country, but I felt like saying, "Soon you can read my book!"

Though Alan didn't write group emails or travel guides, he did keep a journal, which even now I have yet to read. In ambassador school, we were warned about such activity: "If you keep a diary or a journal, hide it under lock and key. Somebody could photograph parts of it and use it against you." We never felt any sense of paranoia, however, and were never concerned or suspicious that others were eyeing us. Perhaps this was because we never felt we were divulging sensitive information of any kind. Journaling allowed Alan to record and reflect on this very special time and to maintain a sense of perspective. For me, it was a way to share our lives in Spain and to feel just a bit more connected with the life I'd left behind.

※

AS FUN AS THE HOLAS were to write, and as much as I enjoyed entertaining visitors, I recognized the need to be more proactive about making Spanish friends. It was a challenge: Spain is a very family-oriented country, and on weekends, everybody tends to retreat into their families. Alan and I had each other, and that was great. Sometimes we liked to hunker down on the weekends too, because we needed a break. And we didn't find many couples who went out on weekend dates, like I was accustomed to doing in Boston. They were busy with their families. Weekends aren't the "going out" nights as they are in the United States.

As I had discovered the hard way with the Asociación de Damas Diplomáticas, learning Spanish was helpful for developing Spanish friendships. And it was something that I truly *wanted* to do. As someone who takes pride in her ability to communicate, I really enjoy the ease of a fluid, unselfconscious conversation. When interacting with

Spanish people, the language barrier always seemed to hold me back. A translator facilitated our communication, but it's hard to get traction in a conversation using an intermediary. For example, I was eager to be involved with FEDEPE (the Spanish Federation of Female Directors, Executives, Professionals and Entrepreneurs)—a group dedicated to promoting female businesswomen, entrepreneurs, and leaders. But FEDEPE's president didn't speak English, and my Spanish wasn't proficient enough to form a connection without language help. This barrier limited what we could accomplish together.

Anticipating this reality before we left Boston, Alan and I had hired a Spanish teacher from a local high school to tutor us every Saturday morning. Each hourlong lesson was packed with vocabulary and verb conjugations that were hard to remember. During one session, we learned how to introduce ourselves and to ask how many brothers and sisters someone has. *How silly*, I thought. *Who's going to ask me how many brothers or sisters I have in a conversation?* But during some of my first interactions in Spain, after I introduced myself to someone, that person immediately asked how many siblings I had. I just had to laugh.

I arrived with the ability to ask basic questions, but I wasn't yet confident or practiced enough to buy olives and manchego, or to talk to my hairdresser about the style and color I wanted. I often had to communicate through gestures, smiles, and interpreters. Luckily, everybody who works in the embassy has access to foreign language lessons if he or she needs them, so we soon began private Spanish lessons with a wonderful teacher, Blanca. Alan had his at eight each morning, and I had mine at eleven. Soon, I had gone beyond learning words and verb conjugations, and was learning more about Spanish culture and people. After about a year, I could converse with Blanca about her family and her life at the embassy.

As it turned out, Blanca's father was the US ambassador's driver in the 1950s. What's more, she remembers exactly where she was at during important moments in Spanish history, such as when Franco died in 1975 or on March 11, 2004, when terrorists set off bombs at Atocha train station (the Spanish equivalent of our 9/11). Blanca also shared with me that after twenty-five years of work at the embassy, she was ready to retire. Not the type of person to become inactive, she wanted to devote herself full-time to her church, her community, and teaching English as a second language.

It would be misleading to suggest that my Spanish was amazing—that I could sustain a fluent conversation about people's lives and historical events. Yet after some months, I was competent enough to gain more intimate access to the personal experiences and perspectives of Spaniards. It was much more revealing to experience the bombings that took place at Atocha train station and other locations through Blanca's eyes than it was to read about it from a textbook. And it was also a gift to feel closer to Blanca. Our relationship started out as professional, but it became more familiar and friendly.

Over time, my Spanish improved, helping me feel more at home in my adopted country. In September 2013, on my first trip to Madrid since relocating back to the States, I realized the strides I had made with the language when FEDEPE bestowed on me the prestigious International Woman of the Year Award. Upon receiving this award from Princess Letizia (now Queen Letizia), I gave my acceptance speech in Spanish, barely using the cue cards. My perseverance had clearly paid off.

As I began to bridge the language gap, I also started bridging the cultural gap. As the saying goes, we all put our pants on one leg at a time. But there were things about Spanish culture that I could never fully grasp. I never got used to social events starting so late at night—dinners beginning at the earliest at 9 p.m., but usually at 10 p.m. on weeknights—or the frequency with which Spaniards smoke, or the sport of bullfighting. On the other hand, the Spanish language allowed me to grasp some of the subtleties of friendship, dress, social connection, and family that prevailed in Spain. And it gave me access to the personal lives of everyday people.

One such person was Ana Garcia. Ana became our new Spanish teacher about halfway through our time in Spain, when Blanca retired. In her thirties, Ana was young, hip, and determined to teach us the language. We learned a great deal about her and her family in the process. Ana lived on her own, but each weekend, she spent time visiting her family in Madrid. She told us about cultural festivals, about how she and her friends socialized, about clothing and shoes. A tiny woman, she would always wear heels that were higher than I'd ever dream of wearing. She'd look at my flat shoes and say she'd never dream of wearing *those*. We'd laugh over our differences.

Through our interactions, I also learned that Spanish women don't speak as intimately and share as much as American women do. American women get very emotional—we delve into how we're thinking and feeling. While becoming proficient in Spanish gave me access to Spanish women's lives, I rarely confided in these women by telling them about my homesickness for my daughters or sharing something else that was troubling me. And they never confided in me. The style of my Spanish friendships was just different—with the exception of my friendship with Cristina, who remains one of my closest friends in the world to this day.

My relationship with Cristina developed gradually. When I arrived at the embassy, she was a godsend, helping me finalize menus, giving me advice on Spanish wine pairings, and helping me do routine things, like buy movie tickets and think through restaurant selections. As our relationship progressed, she would join me upstairs in our private quarters, helping me select just the right outfit to match the occasion. To my delight, she was always positive about my wardrobe choices, and she helped me fine-tune my selections based on the formality of the event. We started opening up to one another, sharing our hopes and dreams, and expressing the challenges we faced at the embassy. I became good friends with her husband, Julio; her son, Jorge; and her mother, Araceli. Cristina became a fixture in my days, greeting me every morning with hugs—and kisses for Stella—and seeing if I needed anything.

One day, I asked Cristina where I could buy one of those beautifully embroidered shawls, called a *mantón*, which Spaniards wear on special occasions like *feria*. "You must go to Sevilla," she said. The two of us embarked on a trip to the city together, where I purchased a *mantón* as a memento of my time in Spain, but I also spent some wonderful time with Cristina "off campus," taking carriage rides and enjoying the colorful sites of Sevilla.

More than anything, I treasured my long walks with Cristina through Madrid. She began joining Stella and me for these walks several times a week, and when I was ready to leave Spain, she told me that she had discovered more about Madrid by walking the city with me than she had learned living there for her entire adult life!

Socializing in Spain is also more formal. One never goes to a party or other event in jeans and a sweater. Dressing up is expected. And my social life mostly revolved around dinner parties, which followed even stricter protocol. Alan and I would always be advised as to the dress code, typically dark suits for men and cocktail attire for women. I'd take my seat on the host's right, and Alan on the hostess's right, and others would radiate out from there, their seats dictated by their relative level of political or diplomatic importance. We'd talk to one person and then to another. These occasions were lovely, but they were not conducive to forming the type of friendships to which I was accustomed. And they took place so darn late at night! It was not uncommon for an event to end at one or two in the morning, which required me to be "on" for long periods. I'd have to muster my energy before going to these events, knowing that I would be out late and talking in Spanish, and that I had to be present with everyone.

Eventually, I hit my stride with socializing. Alan and I really connected with Jaime Malet and his wife, Silvia Sorribas, a corporate mergers and acquisition attorney who works for a leading consulting firm. Silvia joined my women's leadership board, and Jaime was a very important link between Alan and the business community. While this friendship was rooted in our shared business interests, the four of us began to socialize informally too, bonding over a shared love of good food. We sampled the latest Argentinian restaurant, and then a hip Asian fusion place. Jaime and Silvia live in Barcelona, and we often would have dinner with them there. They were among the first Spaniards with whom we became real friends. Over time, we were able to share our lives in a deeper, more personal way.

Alan and I also grew close to Karen—the California blonde I had met through the temple—and her husband, Javier. One day, they invited us to their home on the outskirts of Madrid for some barbecue paella. We spent a pleasant and relaxing afternoon there, enjoying the sunshine and casual conversation. While some Americans build homemade pizza ovens in their backyard, Javier used his outdoor oven to roast paella. Cooking paella in this manner, I discovered, turns the rice crunchy, and saturates the shellfish and other vegetable toppings with a tasty charcoal flavor. But the best part was that Alan and I were able to spend time with new friends in a relaxed way that was reminiscent of our times spent with friends in Boston.

During our third and final year in Spain, I finally found myself beginning to relate to more new friends on a deeper level. One friend invited us to join his family on their boat in the Balearic Islands. Spend three days on someone's boat, surrounded by his family, and you'll get to know the person for sure. Aside from the intimacy of such a setting, somehow the open blue vistas and beautiful, distant landscapes allow people to form more meaningful connections. I began to feel more at home and less self-conscious around the embassy and at our adopted temple, too.

Alan had felt comfortable in Spain from the beginning. In fact, from the moment he heard we were headed to Spain, he had gone full steam ahead, making sure he got the most out of every minute of this adventure. It took me more time to develop the experience, knowledge, and confidence to feel comfortable and settled. Part of that was finding a sense of balance in who I was, how I spent my time, and the role I fulfilled. As I learned how to be more authentic in my role, and how to do more than just smile and look lovingly at my husband, I found I could enjoy other people more. I became more patient with the "otherness" of the Spaniards I met—and I no longer judged every relationship against the yardstick of my love for friends back home.

❦

AFTER ALL THE TIME AND energy I had spent feeling lonely and missing our friends, you'd think that upon our return to the United States, I would've spent all my time socializing and catching up on relationships. I didn't. Rather, I retreated, and so did Alan.

As Alan and I planned our return to Boston, a friend asked if she could throw us a "welcome home" party. We politely declined. Enough of big parties and social events! We wanted to connect with friends on a close, intimate, one-on-one basis. The last thing we wanted was to attend another party or large social event in our honor.

Nor did I want to bump into anyone at the local supermarket; I dreaded the inevitable "welcome home" conversation and rehashing the highlights of my time abroad. I just wanted to slip back into my life from before Spain. Though I didn't realize it at the time, this was my attempt to slow down our lives and take stock of things. I just needed to enjoy some peace and quiet—to be with myself, with Alan, and with a few special friends, so that I could process everything we'd been through.

We saw almost all our closest friends within the first month of being home. They came over for a casual barbecue dinner or joined us for a dinner out so we could sit and talk. My intention was to simplify. This was the third promise Alan had made to me before leaving for Spain: that when we returned, we would lead a simpler life. Truth be told, simplifying our lives is still a work in progress. But when we first returned, "simplification" meant spending quality time with friends and really experiencing a slow, balanced lifestyle.

Three years later, I'm still catching up with friends. I'll bump into people who say they haven't seen me since we left for Spain and want to know all about my experience. "What an amazing time you must have had!" they often say.

"Yes," I reply, telling them parts of the story. Now that I've had time to process what the experience meant to me, I've generated more of an "elevator speech" about it. I'm able to convey what a life-changing, extraordinary time I had in Spain without getting into details about the day-to-day or the challenges I faced while there. Time puts a very positive shine on it all, naturally. As I reminisce about my experience abroad and share it with others, whether in passing or more deeply, I'm able to bask in all the wonderful moments and appreciate the extraordinary opportunity Alan and I were given. My friendships are incredibly dear to me, and I really value them more and more as time moves on. But I've also tried to cherish and reserve the time that I need to recharge and renew myself. This is something that comes easier for me than for Alan.

My current involvement as a trustee with the Berklee College of Music is a good example. Founded in 1945 and based in Boston, Berklee is a leading international contemporary music school. Soon after the 2008 election, Berklee president Roger Brown paid Alan a visit. Roger and his wife, Linda Mason, are entrepreneurs who had started an amazing company before Roger decided to change course and embark on a whole new path in academia. He and Alan, both leaders in the New England Steering Committee that helped elect President Obama, had gotten together that day to talk about fundraising. When Roger explained that Berklee was expanding abroad, planning to build a Mediterranean campus in Valencia, Spain, Alan discreetly mentioned that he was being considered to represent President Obama in Spain. Roger was eager to get us involved in the expansion effort, and persuaded me to join the Berklee Valencia Advisory Board. Because I adore music and the arts, it was an ideal position for me.

When Alan was confirmed as ambassador and we moved to Spain, we became involved with the Valencia expansion. Various singers, songwriters, and musicians, including Berklee students and faculty, gave musical performances at US embassy events. Berklee officially opened the Valencia campus while we were abroad, and I visited the Valencia campus in my official capacity as an advisory member. Located in the Ciudad de las Artes y las Ciencias in a *Jetsons*-style building designed by architect Santiago Calatrava, the Valencia campus is just as vibrant as its sister college and the city of Boston. When I returned home from Spain, Roger asked me to join Berklee's board of trustees, and I agreed. It's been a wonderfully fulfilling role ever since.

My involvement with Berklee really bookended my trip to Spain. But in a way, it is also reflective of my new attitude toward life. Before leaving for Spain, I was involved in many such activities, but upon my return, I learned to say no to things as well. I agreed to become a trustee at Berklee simply because I knew I would find it so fulfilling. During my three years on the board, I've had a wonderful time hearing music, engaging with substantive issues facing the campus and the larger community, and developing relationships with other board members in a smart, thoughtful atmosphere where everyone's input is valued.

Of course, learning to say no has been a process, and it's not always easy. But that doesn't bother me. I no longer rush to do everything. Although I have many things going on, I'm careful not to overburden myself. In Spain, I experienced fanfare, pomp, and circumstance—and the struggle to find a place for myself in a different cultural environment. Now, I just want to be my "normal" self. I'm careful to stay grounded. I focus on quality over quantity, and derive the most meaning possible from what I do. My days are precious to me, and I want to control how I fill them.

During our time in Spain, I returned periodically to the United States—perhaps once every three to four months. Each time, I would make plans to meet my dearest friends. By the time the plane landed, we'd have dates scheduled to see one another. Alan gave this time a beautiful name: "the warm embrace of home." When Alan and I finally moved back home, we got off the plane and made the ritual calls. This time I told my friends, "We're back for good."

We really had traveled from the mountains of Madrid to the coast of Barcelona. Now we were home, in our leafy Boston suburb, surrounded by the friends we loved. That warm embrace was back for good too. And it felt great.

EIGHT

"WHAT A LONG STRANGE TRIP IT'S BEEN"—AND STILL IS

A S OUR THIRD YEAR IN Spain drew to a close, it was time to begin planning for our return to the United States. This was only natural. Noncareer ambassadors like Alan usually leave their post after a new presidential term begins. If Mitt Romney had won the 2012 presidential election, Alan would have tendered his resignation, effective January 20, 2013—Inauguration Day. But with Obama winning reelection in 2012, we had some flexibility in planning our departure.

It benefits incumbent presidents such as Obama for ambassadors to linger a bit in their country and position after an election cycle, providing time for the appointment of a new ambassador. Eduardo Aguirre, Alan's predecessor, always offered us good advice and he advised us to control the departure as much as possible. Once again, it was good advice.

As 2013 unfolded, I found that I was ready to return home. As much as I had grown to love Spain, I yearned for a place where everything was familiar. I longed to return to my old routines and to enjoy deep and dear connections with friends and family. I craved the ease of communicating solely in English and of always knowing my way around. By winter's end, I was ready to leave and thought the end of March would be ideal. But I knew that Alan would seek to stay longer—that if he had the option, he probably would never leave Spain.

Would Alan and I find a way to agree on a date for our final departure?

In January 2013, we departed on one of our typical weekend trips to explore more of Spain. We visited the small, scenic town of Sigüenza, located about an hour and a half north of Madrid. Sigüenza boasts a beautiful Gothic cathedral begun in the twelfth century, a medieval castle, and the remnants of ancient Roman walls. As we wound our way through the countryside with Enrique at the wheel, I was struck by an idea. I turned to Alan and whispered, "Let's stay in Spain until the beginning of summer. However, I have one condition: in February, let's take another trip to Morocco."

A few months earlier, in November 2012, Alan and I had celebrated our twenty-eighth anniversary by taking a short vacation to Marrakech, Morocco. Though only a two-hour plane ride from Madrid, Morocco was like entering a completely different world. Towering minarets and elegant mosques announced the call to prayer five times a day; pedestrian traffic halted as people positioned their mats on the ground facing east and prayed to Allah. As we walked, the streets enveloped us in scents of saffron, turmeric, and cumin. Women all around us wore hijabs or burqas, and men wore leathery, pointed sandals in vivid blues, yellows, and purples.

In town squares, snake charmers enchanted crowds and the rhythms of traditional Berber music filled the open air. The buildings were low and adobe-colored, providing a respite from the strong Sahara sunshine and the bustle of the busy, open-air marketplaces. Wandering through these enclosures, we marveled at the intricate carvings and ceramic tiles, bathed in North Africa's bright signature greens and yellows. Adding to the magic, no security detail or staff accompanied us when we were out of the country. Alan and I were completely alone at last.

Five days didn't allow us to really get to know this striking country, but it piqued my curiosity and sparked my imagination. Soon, I was falling in love with exotic Morocco and wondered when we could possibly return there. As I told Alan on our way to Sigüenza, another visit to Morocco meant we could visit the city of Fez and further explore the Saharan desert and other sites.

Alan didn't hesitate. "It's a deal!" he exclaimed.

We were both relieved by this decision, and the departure date made good, practical sense. In Spain, business and social life slow during the summer. Many people head to the beach or go abroad for rest and relaxation. If we left at the end of June, we could bring the year's business to a natural close and say our final goodbyes before people departed for vacation. We could even host our annual Fourth of July celebration at the embassy and use that as an opportunity to bid farewell to the many, many friends we had made. This date also gave us enough time to plan and organize several additional farewell events. I looked forward to preparing my various embassy initiatives for the next administration. Alan, true to form, had a dizzying number of initiatives he sought to conclude as well.

We couldn't announce our departure date until it was close. Alan didn't want to assume the status of "lame duck" ambassador, just waiting to exit. That was not his style at all. Although I understood that it was better not to announce prematurely, I also hate keeping secrets. Plus, I was not looking forward to saying our goodbyes.

※

BEFORE BEGINNING THE SEASON OF farewells and final events, we took that trip Alan had promised, flying to Marrakech in February 2013. A driver from our hotel met us at the airport and ferried us across the Atlas Mountains into the Valley of One Thousand Kasbahs—the most impressive of the oasis valleys in southern Morocco. The driver maneuvered us fearlessly through the small, winding roads for four hours, taking us past carts, wagons, horses, and Bedouins traveling to their next location. My heart sank into my stomach as he made sharp hairpin turns, navigating steep, downhill descents with no shoulder on the road to protect us should something go wrong.

I had carefully researched our itinerary, choosing a small boutique hotel that felt utterly foreign and exotic. Once there, our hotel arranged for us to take an overnight excursion to the edge of the Saharan desert. I kept imagining *Lawrence of Arabia*, with unending landscapes of dunes and sand and deep blue skies without a single cloud—and not much else.

Our accommodations were described as a "desert tent," but that portrayal is misleading. The "tent" was ultra-luxurious, equipped with lights, running water, and even a makeshift toilet. Beautiful Berber carpets covered the ground, and artwork adorned the walls. Best of all, Alan and I were alone in the North African desert. No security vehicles or personnel loomed in the distance, as they had on other trips. With zero internet connectivity, we savored the feeling of being detached from modern life, surrounded by endless sand dunes, punctuated every so often by a camel caravan. Even though we were there for less than twenty-four hours, we were still at the mercy of the elements—the evening was cold, and the daytime sweltering.

After settling in, we took a walk along the dunes. As the sky grew darker, the staff met us at our tent and announced that they were there to guide us to dinner. We walked down a sand dune lit by hurricane lanterns and candles, still becoming accustomed to the Sahara's barrenness. Lo and behold, we were led to a bonfire over which pots of lamb stew simmered. We enjoyed a glorious, four-course meal, entranced by millions of stars sparkling overhead. The next morning, the staff woke us before dawn, provided us with hot coffee and fresh orange juice, and encouraged us to go outside to watch the sunrise. It's hard to convey how amazing it is to watch the sun slowly illuminate a desert landscape. We returned to our hotel via another five-hour drive and took in the mystical land of centuries-old fortresses—the One Thousand Kasbahs.

After this short sojourn, we flew to Casablanca and, of course, visited Rick's Café, a replica of the establishment made famous in the classic film *Casablanca,* starring Humphrey Bogart and Ingrid Bergman. An American expat now owns and operates the place. We spent some time with her and learned that she came to Morocco as a commercial foreign service officer, fell in love with the country, and has stayed there ever since. We could understand that path in life, even if it wouldn't be ours.

Making our way to Rabat, where the US embassy is located, we visited with our friends, ambassador Sam Kaplan and his wife, Sylvia. The Kaplans hail from Minnesota and had occupied their post for around the same amount of time as we had. Like us, they had approached their mission as a partnership, although Sylvia had taken her role as the ambassador's wife in a different direction than I had. When she entertained at her home, she took over the kitchen and cooked for everyone. Judging from the dozens of tagine pots she had around her kitchen, she *loved* Moroccan cuisine and hosting, just as I had loved my women's leadership series and my philanthropic and volunteer initiatives. We had chosen different paths. She had roots in political activism, and expressed her deep political values and beliefs in one way; I was a businesswoman from New England and chose to make my time meaningful in another way. Each approach best suited our respective passions and personalities.

After visiting the Kaplans, we rounded off our trip with a visit to the UNESCO heritage city of Fez. We savored the exotic spices; the winding roads; the narrow alleys lined with shops; the Jewish Quarter, which included a synagogue; and the sounds of Muslim calls to prayer. We then returned to Spain, refreshed and ready to finish our work—and to prepare for our farewells and departure.

As it turned out, some of our farewells proved to be joyous events; others were bittersweet, even painful. All of them, however, enabled us to make the transition we needed, putting the final stamp on this exciting three-and-a-half-year adventure. They also enabled me to think more deeply about what we had experienced and how we had changed.

One of my most enjoyable tasks during this final period was delivering the commencement address at St. Louis University in Madrid. Our daughter Stephanie was about to graduate from college in the United States, so it was a special honor for me to help these Spanish and international students mark the completion of their college years. I used my speech as a chance to reflect on my time in Spain—ushering these students into the world as I prepared to usher myself from the fairy-tale land of Oz back to the proverbial farmhouse in Kansas.

Instead of giving the standard "follow your dreams" speech, I took a slightly different route, emphasizing that life is "a long and winding road." As I told these young people, they *should* follow their dreams, realizing as well that life could deliver twists and turns that would deal them unexpected setbacks and challenges.

Where I might have differed from the standard commencement speaker was my decision to share some honest truths about my own life. As I told the audience, when I graduated from Cornell—at the same life stage as the audience before me—I drifted a bit, unsure of what I wanted out of life. I traveled to San Francisco to teach kindergarten, only to find that it wasn't my true calling. I eventually took a hard look at myself, asking some difficult questions. It took me a while to find my way in business, and I was forced to accept that life wasn't a linear progression. I learned that I needed to seize every opportunity that came my way, even if it wasn't exactly what I had anticipated.

I went on to describe some of the story told in this book—how I struggled initially with living in Spain, and how I carved out a new role for myself as the ambassador's wife, focusing on women, entrepreneurship, and volunteerism. As I related, I had managed to create a new dream for myself. These remarks came from my heart, and they served, much as this book does, as a way of bidding Spain a meaningful farewell.

Back at the embassy, I concentrated on wrapping up my cherished initiatives. My final women's leadership event, which took place in June 2013, dealt with entrepreneurial ventures, a major focus of Alan's and the embassy's attention. Shortly after I had arrived in Spain, entrepreneur and business leader María Benjumea had asked me to join the board of the Spain Startup & Investor Summit (Spain Startup). María had long been aware of Spain's shortage of entrepreneurial energy, and she was determined to do something about it. With her unending passion, drive, creativity, and leadership, she founded and led Spain Startup, an annual summit that brought together some of Spain's great innovators and shined a light on the country's impressive pool of talent. Given how much María had contributed to the cause of Spanish entrepreneurship, I thought her a perfect choice for our concluding women's leadership event.

Initially, I had been reluctant to serve on Spain Startup's advisory board, concerned that I lacked entrepreneurial experience. But I eventually agreed—and thankfully so. Spain Startup's annual events were a huge success throughout my time in Spain, driven by María's high-energy personality. At my first Startup Summit, I arrived expecting to see one hundred or so attendees, but attendance topped one thousand, including prominent business leaders and government officials. That number swelled in subsequent years.

Five entrepreneurs spoke at each session, with each allowed ten minutes to describe his or her activities. The format was reminiscent of speed dating, with companies making pitches and trying to court potential clients, and the presentations were amazing. One year, a speaker described an exciting new vest for motorcyclists that his organization had engineered. The back of the vest came equipped with LED lights to signal left, right, and stop. The idea struck me as an ingenious and logical way to prevent the motorcycle accidents and deaths that occur with haunting frequency on Spanish streets and highways.

During the same morning presentation, I was privileged to watch a ten-year-old boy talk about his budding adventures in entrepreneurship. Small and slight, he appeared on the big stage dressed in grey flannel shorts, a blue Oxford shirt, a button-down sweater, and knee-high socks, resembling the title character from the Frances Hodgson Burnett novel *Little Lord Fauntleroy*. Much to everyone's surprise, this young man was poised and professional, leading the crowd through a polished PowerPoint presentation. He began by describing a terrible problem: his pencil case tended to fall over at school, sending pencils flying around his classroom and angering his teachers. Determined to overcome this problem, he had assembled a team of his fourth-grade classmates. One person oversaw marketing and advertising while others took care of research and development. This little boy's meticulous presentation featured a pencil case system that would remain upright and keep pencils intact—no more chaotic classrooms and unhappy teachers. This presentation confirmed that an entrepreneurial mindset *did* exist among Spanish youth. Today, it's a new pencil case. Tomorrow, who knows—perhaps a successor to Facebook.

When the embassy's head of public diplomacy alerted me that Esther Aguilera, who heads the US Congressional Hispanic Caucus Institute (CHCI), would be visiting Madrid in June 2013 as part of CHCI's effort to promote entrepreneurship, I recognized it as great timing. Our final women's leadership event would feature not one but two powerhouses. The embassy was as excited about it as I was, a marked shift from earlier in my tenure when I had to fight to get embassy officials to support my ideas. *Of course these events are valuable*, the prevailing mindset seemed to be. I felt as if I had furthered a cause—women's business leadership—that mattered to me. I hoped this series of events would continue long after I left.

As anticipated, María and Esther were marvelous. At the end of the event, María, in her creative and characteristically unorthodox way, stood up and announced, "Susan, we have a gift for you!" She brought forth a large leg of the country's signature *jamón ibérico*, draped in a Spanish flag. The thing was massive—three feet long and weighing about fifty pounds. Maria formally presented the Spanish delicacy to me as a gesture of friendship and goodwill. The audience roared with laughter and applause. Embassy staff quickly ushered the *jamón* into the kitchen for slicing and sharing. It was such a sweet gesture. I realized that these special touches and thoughtful acts were part of what had made my time in Spain so rich.

In addition to promoting women's leadership and entrepreneurship, Alan and I had devoted a lot of our time at the embassy to encouraging volunteerism. We therefore planned a large community service day to bid farewell at the embassy. For this half-day event, called Amigos Para Siempre ("Friends Forever"), we visited different neighborhoods in Madrid, painting buildings, working in schools, and spending time with senior citizens and mentally challenged young adults. The work was meaningful and connecting.

It was a gorgeous, sunny summer day, and we capped off the festivities back at the embassy with a barbecue on our front lawn. We had purchased T-shirts that read *Amigos Para Siempre* and gave them to everyone. We reminisced about the many occasions we had shared together. The embassy employees presented us with goodbye gifts, honoring Alan with a flag that had flown that day over the embassy and me with a painting of one of the *meninas* that I had collected. We were also given three huge volumes of press clippings that catalogued our time in Spain. These expressions of affection brought tears to my eyes. We had lived and worked with our embassy colleagues and had forged strong friendships. Their commitment and devotion to strengthening US–Spain relationships ran deep, but their friendship touched us even more deeply. It pained me to realize we would no longer see them every day.

꿏

THE PINNACLE EVENT MARKING OUR departure was our final Fourth of July celebration at the embassy. I had arrived in Spain with minimal understanding of the importance of these events or their purpose. Over time, as I had familiarized myself with our role and responsibility in our host country, I developed a much firmer grasp on how a US embassy properly marks the Fourth of July. And this year, although our celebration would be held on June 24, I was determined to make it truly special.

Working with an embassy committee, we invited three thousand guests, including government, business, and community leaders as well as close personal friends of ours and of the embassy. We tried to reach out to everyone who had touched us or whom we had touched during our time in Spain. Music was paramount. Alicia, a talented Spanish woman who worked at the embassy and had impressed us with her extraordinary vocal range over the previous few years, agreed to sing

"The Star-Spangled Banner." We also invited several bands to play American classics on multiple stages. Finally, I knew that Alan and I would each speak, and that we would both deliver our speeches entirely in Spanish.

The event was everything I had hoped it would be. Alan and I danced for hours. Friends and acquaintances stopped to hug and kiss us and recall shared memories. At the height of the evening, Alan and I joined the band onstage, fulfilling my dream of being a rock 'n' roll singer (even for just a night). Together, we sang the Beatles' "Hey Jude" before the large crowd. Never in my life had I done such a thing! High up on the stage, I felt jubilant. But my speech was an even bigger moment—my personal *enhorabuena*. I had worked so hard to learn Spanish, and now I took great pride in my ability to competently and confidently speak in public, with a strong vocabulary, easier pronunciation, and better delivery.

The Fourth of July celebration was the grandest of many memorable goodbyes. But there were others leading up to it.

We were invited to Palacio de la Zarzuela for a farewell audience with their royal majesties, el Rey Juan Carlos and la Reina Sofia, and when we arrived, I had yet another "pinch me" moment. There I was at the Zarzuela Palace, the home of Spain's royal family. The royal household had allotted twenty to thirty minutes for the visit, but we ended up staying for well over an hour. The queen expressed her sadness at our departure and her love for President Obama, while the king lobbed question after question, asking about our final impressions of his country, where we were going, and what we had most enjoyed during our tenure. He delivered high praise, telling us how well we had represented the United States. Following our visit with the king and queen, we were set to meet with Crown Prince Felipe and Princess Letizia. Our audience took so long that we kept the prince and princess waiting, and they were delayed in greeting the son of the emperor of Japan. Nonetheless, they, too, were warm and engaging, and we took photos to commemorate the occasion.

The afternoon was slipping away, and upon departing from Zarzuela, we had to rush back to the embassy for my farewell women's luncheon. Alan instructed Enrique to flash the blue lights and siren so we could speed through the capital. Even so, I arrived to find a hundred women already seated for lunch. Ana Botella, the mayor of Madrid, was in attendance, as were panelists from my women's leadership forums, guests I had featured at philanthropy roundtables, journalists who had interviewed me, and dear friends who had welcomed us to their homes for *copitas* and dinner parties. I was pleased to find I could personally identify each and every attendee—who she was, what she did, how we had connected, and how we planned, plotted, and enjoyed friendship and laughter over the years. As I entered the room, everyone rose to their feet and clapped for me.

After lunch, something even more amazing happened. One woman started to sing, and soon the whole room joined in. The song was in Spanish, and everyone seemed to know the words. The title, "Algo Se Muere en el Alma Cuando un Amiga Se Va," translates to "something in your soul dies when a friend leaves." The lyrics go on to convey heartfelt thanks to a friend. One hundred amazing, inspirational women were publicly acknowledging my efforts in Spain and demonstrating how much I would be missed. I was speechless. I doubt I will ever again experience such a humbling, thoughtful, and grand gesture of friendship!

Time was running out. June 28, our departure date, was drawing near. The packing began, and we girded ourselves for some of the most emotional goodbyes of all.

One day, a few weeks before we left, the residence staff gathered for lunch in the staff dining room, just as they always did. In that room—a small, fluorescent-lit space on the residence's ground floor, bordering a large industrial-sized kitchen—Alan and I did our best to acknowledge the staff members' roles in our lives and to thank each individual personally for everything she or he had done on our behalf.

The love and respect we shared was genuine and heartfelt. Eight of the nine staff members did not speak English very well, but over the years, my broken Spanish had become stronger, as had their English comprehension. We had learned how Carlos the footman had worked diligently for the US embassy for seventeen years, supporting his family in Ecuador, and how Ani the maid worked to support her family in Paraguay. We had come to know Adelina, whose sweet emotions could make her (and therefore me) tear up at anything even slightly sentimental. Antonio the butler had spent a large part of the Franco regime unjustly imprisoned simply for being gay, but you wouldn't ever know it from the way he smiled through all his past hardship. He had dedicated himself to keeping us organized, and his commitment to thoughtful details—like making sure the residence had the most beautiful floral arrangements—had helped Alan and me feel at home.

Saying goodbye to these extraordinary people, who felt like family, was tremendously hard. Never again would a group of people attend to me with such love, care, and devotion. We had gifts for each of them, but perhaps the most meaningful one was the American flag that Alan presented to Cristina. It had flown over the embassy and was identical to the triangular flags encased in gift boxes that Alan gave to important embassy guests and visiting dignitaries. The entire staff was deeply touched. No previous ambassador had ever made such a gesture to a member of the residence staff. We felt strongly that these hardworking men and women, who helped us, cared for us, and loved us, should be rightly recognized for their service.

Cristina merited her own, individual farewell. She was my dearest friend in Spain, the person who sat me down again and again to coach me through the formalities of my role and the intricacies of Spanish culture and daily life. When I felt completely defeated by Spain's banking system, she offered to help deposit my check. When I needed the right dress for a fancy cocktail party, I could count on her good taste. When I drove a car in Spain for the first time, Cristina sat next to me and taught me how to navigate the streets of Madrid. When Stella needed to go to the vet, Cristina offered to come along so I wouldn't get lost. I could fill pages and pages extolling Cristina's virtues and detailing how meaningful and dear she is to me.

For three and a half years, I saw Cristina every single weekday, from eight in the morning until six at night. What started as a purely business relationship morphed into a deep friendship. Just like American girlfriends, we started talking about personal matters, including our husbands, children, parents, weekend plans, and life in general. Yet despite our familiarity, Cristina never called me anything but "Madam." Even after we left, and she came to visit me in Boston, she couldn't kick the habit of addressing me in this way. Try as I might, I could not persuade her to call me Susan.

Once, in Boston, I took her to Bloomingdale's, and as we shopped, I heard a Spanish-accented voice echo through the department store: "Madam, come look at this!" Heads turned in surprise, and I could only chuckle. I'm thrilled to report that today, Cristina calls me Susan, and we remain dear friends despite the ocean that separates us. Her son was recently accepted to Emerson College in Boston, and I'm excited about the prospect of seeing her more often.

Alan felt that these goodbyes were becoming overwhelming, and that perhaps we needed a break. I agreed, so in mid-June we flew to France to visit our friends, Ambassador Charlie Rivkin and his wife, Susan Tolson. The US embassy in Paris has a rich history, and staying there was quite an honor. Alan and I had a lot of free time to roam Paris and enjoy its beauty and culture, its museums, parks, and restaurants.

We also accompanied Charlie and Susan to an official event, a black-tie gala at the Palace of Versailles, hosted by the American Friends of Versailles. We mingled with American Francophiles in long evening gowns and tuxedos as fireworks burst above us at the stroke of midnight.

When Alan and I returned from the weekend, we traveled about the country saying goodbye to others who had touched us. Over the years, Alan and I visited the American consulate office in Barcelona frequently. We worked closely with the consul general and the consulate staff, and we were familiar with various Barcelona-based businesses, cultural institutions, and government officials. Visiting Barcelona was always fun, and we especially loved the city's stunning architecture, framed by mountains and bathed in the Mediterranean's sunshine and sparkle.

Consul General Tanya Anderson and the consulate staff hosted yet another farewell party in our honor. During their planning, they had quietly contacted me to choose a song with which to serenade Alan during the party. "What song would be most meaningful to him?" they asked.

Answering wasn't hard. I suggested "Somewhere Over the Rainbow," from the movie *The Wizard of Oz*, to conjure up our adventure in this magical land. Gwen Perry, an American expat and professional singer living in Barcelona, sang the song *a cappella* for Alan. Usually the stoic and steady ambassador, Alan couldn't hold back the tears.

Our next farewell trip took us south and east, to the Balearic Islands. People often ask about my favorite place in Spain, and I usually say, "Everywhere. Put me anywhere in Spain, and I'll be very happy." If pressed, however, I might have to go with the Balearics. Mallorca, Menorca, and Ibiza—the three principle destinations in this island chain—offer long stretches of beautiful, white sandy beaches; an occasional black sand beach; jagged mountains; quaint fishing villages; and green, rolling hills dotted with olive trees and vineyards. During our final trip, Alan and I had business to conduct, but we also planned to treat ourselves to an extra day or two for rest and relaxation.

We kicked off the trip in Mallorca's capital city of Palma attending an official event that commemorated the three hundredth anniversary of the birth of Father Junípero Serra. A monk born in Mallorca, Serra traveled to the American southwest where he founded a string of Catholic missions in present-day California. Although somewhat controversial in the United States, he is revered in his home region. The ceremony we attended was held in a centuries-old cathedral and included music, candlelight, and speeches proclaiming Spain's historic relationship with America.

After this, our private time began, and Alan and I ventured inland to stay at a wonderful boutique hotel nestled in the Mallorcan hills. We accepted a kind offer to join friends for several days on their boat moored in Ibiza. I had pictured staying on one of those massive cabin cruisers that resembles a mansion on the water; we had seen hundreds of them docked in Mallorca's harbor. To my delight, after our hosts met us in the Ibizan harbor town of Eivissa, we motored out to a sleek sailboat about one hundred meters long, with tall masts that caught the wind. Can you say *heaven*?

During the day, we sailed around Ibiza and Formentera, a small island to the south. At night, we enjoyed marvelous sit-down dinners with fresh fish, salads, cocktails, and wonderful conversation among friends. Since we were still in Spain, Alan required security. This time, however, it was limited to a Spanish coast guard boat that followed us at a distance. More privacy for us, and not a bad assignment for those guys.

Before I knew it, our time in Spain was drawing to a close. The night before our final departure for the United States—after all the good-bye parties, the farewell to royalty, the final luncheons, our last travels, a day of volunteerism, and the Fourth of July celebration—Alan surprised me with a dinner for just the two of us. Our dear Chef Gustavo prepared an assortment of our favorite dishes. Alan had menus printed that described the meal as the "Somewhere Over the Rainbow Dinner."

We began with Gustavo's famous infused spherical olives *aceitunas esféricas*, tuna tartare, and paella served with a shot of delightfully spicy gazpacho. All of this was paired with a dry Freixenet Cava, which tingled on our lips and complemented the food's sophisticated notes. Next was Gustavo's deconstructed *tortilla española*. The main course was grilled salmon accompanied by a white asparagus, corn, and tomato salad, and it was followed by a cheese plate. We topped off the meal with Oreo cookies—not just any Oreo cookies, but Gustavo's handmade cookie logs suffused with flavors.

It occurred to me during dinner that while ambassador school had prepared us to arrive in Madrid, it had provided no instructions about how to depart from our post. Alan and I weren't just saying goodbye to casual friends, we were leaving a cast of characters—the Scarecrow, the Tin Man, the Lion—all special people who had helped us learn, grow, and do good work during our time in this enchanting land of Oz. We were following our own instincts and hearts in saying goodbye, doing what felt right in the moment.

※

WHEN ALAN AND I AWOKE the next morning, we found that June 28 had arrived. Every step was laced with sadness. The movers had packed and removed all our belongings, leaving us in an empty residence with nothing on the walls, no books or tchotchkes lining the bookshelves, no clothing assembled in the closets. The barren shelves and walls left us feeling lonely, empty, and hollow. I still have a picture of Alan and I sitting in our empty living room, dejected looks on our faces. We were no longer just talking about leaving. Our day of departure had finally arrived.

The saddest and most poignant moment of all was Stella Blu's final goodbye. At ten thirty in the morning, a few hours before we left for the airport, our "ambassadog" was scheduled for her own private transport to the airport. The staff at the residence all loved Stella, but Antonio the butler had developed the closest relationship with her. He spoke to her in Spanish, and she understood everything he said, following him everywhere, trotting at his heels as he carried out his duties. It was fitting that he bring Stella to the car.

Dressed in his butler uniform, with those striped pants and a crisply pressed, shortened black jacket, Antonio carried Stella to the back of my Volvo, gently placing her crate in the hatchback, giving her loving head rubs and kisses. Unaware of what was happening, Stella looked totally confused. Antonio stopped to embrace her, put her in the car, and then walked away, sobbing. I watched the scene from the second-floor window—the one heartbreaking goodbye I could bear to watch only from a distance. To this day, I still mourn the fact that Stella will never see her dear friend Antonio again.

An hour later, we got the call: "Mr. Ambassador, your car is ready to take you and Mrs. Solomont to the airport." Alan's black limo was waiting in front of the residence, just as it always was. Enrique was set to drive us, and Alan's entire security team was assembled out front, ready for our farewell. I didn't even try to be strong as the tears streamed down my face. These men, and one woman, had traveled everywhere with us for three and a half years. Despite our language differences, we had forged deep connections and enjoyed a wonderful set of memories. I loved every one of these people. We stopped to take a photo, and then Alan and I settled into our usual seats: Alan on the right, me on the left.

Watching the now familiar city whirl past, we held hands and were speechless with emotion. Instead of seeking out the right words to say, I turned on my phone and played a song that captured what we were feeling—a tune by The Byrds written by Roger McGuinn, that celebrates the spirit of a love that never dies:

> *I'm gonna hold you right here in my arms as the limousine*
> *takes us away,*
> *And we'll dream about the music of some brighter day.*

Yes, the limousine was taking us away—but the days ahead of us would be every bit as bright as the ones we had lived in Spain.

At the airport, Alan's senior team awaited us, along with Cristina and our wonderful friend, Marta Soriano, the head of protocol. We filed into the same VIP room where we'd first arrived three and a half years earlier. While I felt so close to everyone in the room, I also felt overwhelmed. How many times could we say goodbye? Unfortunately, even this goodbye dragged on as the plane was delayed. We hung out, making small talk to pass the time—although in truth, I think Alan was still talking policy.

Finally, the plane was ready, and it was time for the *final* goodbye, replete with kisses, hugs, and tears. We were ushered into a van and driven onto the tarmac. Just like in the movies, we climbed a set of stairs, our carry-on luggage in tow. The plane's Spanish pilot stood waiting at the top of the staircase, offering a formal greeting to the outgoing US ambassador and his wife. He thanked us for our years of service and escorted us to our seats. We were the last to board, and by the time we settled in, the plane began to taxi.

Holding my hand, Alan turned to me and said, "We're leaving Oz. Time to go back to Kansas." The doors shut, and we took off, watching as the magical land receded below us.

During the eight-hour flight home, Alan and I busied ourselves reading and looking through pictures on our computers. As the plane began its descent over Massachusetts, we glimpsed the outlines of Cape Cod, from the elbow to the tip of Provincetown. I prepared myself for landing, marveling at how green and familiar the landscape appeared. Much of Spain is dry, dusty, and brown. Now, everything was back in color, the greens of summer.

We used our diplomatic passports one last time, making our way through security before retrieving our suitcases and our most precious piece of cargo—sweet Stella. I had thought about having her fly in the cabin with us, but in the cargo compartment, she always managed just fine.

I think our daughter Becca picked us up from the airport that day, but honestly, I can't recall. All I remember is walking into the house, thinking, *Oh my God, we're home.*

To my utter surprise, Stella hadn't lost her bearings at all. After so many years away, she knew exactly where to find her bowl, her sleeping mats, and her food. Her transition was seamless. For the rest of us, everything felt familiar but also slightly strange. There was an eerie silence and finality to coming home. We weren't just visiting, as we had on several occasions. Our return was permanent, and we knew it.

As Alan had said to me when we stepped off the plane, "We're not in Oz anymore."

❧

NOW THAT I WAS AT home, a host of questions popped up: *What do I do? How should I spend my time? Who am I now?* I needed to settle back into my "old" life, but really, it was a new life. I was excited to resume normal and even mundane tasks like cooking breakfast, running errands, driving places, doing the laundry, making plans. For the first time in three and a half years, Alan and I needn't adhere to a strict schedule devised with the help of others. We wouldn't have bodyguards, nor would we enjoy the assistance of a devoted team. The onus was on us to ensure that daily life unfolded in a meaningful, productive, and enjoyable way.

Within a few days, I realized that much had changed during our absence. The major landmarks in our neighborhood and city remained, of course, but life had gone on. Familiar shops and restaurants had closed, and new ones had opened. Friends had celebrated milestones in their lives without us. New faces appeared at our familiar organizations and on charitable boards.

Most significantly, I had changed as well.

A few weeks after returning, I had breakfast with my former boss, Peter Karoff. As we sat having breakfast at a local restaurant, he offered reassuring words: "Susan, it seems like you've moved on and gone beyond much of what you did in the past. You're going to do new and different things now. You're going to spread your wings again."

His comments startled me. Had I changed that much? How had I "moved on"? I wondered if my old employer, The Philanthropic Initiative, didn't want me back, and Peter was trying to let me down easy. I chose to interpret his words as wise counsel and well-meaning advice, coming from a man whom I deeply admired. In the wake of that breakfast, I found myself wondering: If I had moved beyond something, where exactly had I landed?

I struggled mightily with this question. Since the State Department hadn't clearly defined the role of an ambassador's spouse, I had enjoyed the mixed blessing of a relatively blank slate. I'd worked on carving out a space for myself beyond the standard smiling, doting spouse. But more than that, I had reoriented myself in midlife, charting a new course in a very deliberate and proactive way. Now that I was back home, I needed to continue this project. Instead of simply defining my role as the ambassador's spouse, I needed to think in terms of my *life*.

With my children grown and out of the house, with a successful career now behind me, what did I want to accomplish? Had I "retired"?

The word itself makes me uncomfortable. In its original sense, it means "to withdraw" or "to turn away." But in my case, retirement has come to mean a very selective and conscious process of turning *toward* certain activities and goals—ones that are especially meaningful to me.

I began to assess what activities and pursuits would make me happiest and most fulfilled. In the abstract, striking out in new directions sounded refreshing and wonderful, but in practice, it's tough. An obvious option was to return part-time to TPI and contribute my energy to causes and institutions that I loved. But heeding Peter's advice and knowing I had a rare opportunity, I decided on a different path. If Spain taught me anything, it was that I needed to challenge myself. I didn't want to pick up where I left off. I wanted to continue growing, expand my horizons, and try new things.

Although a work in progress, the life that I've carved out for myself since returning from Spain has transcended the usual labels and categories. I no longer define myself by my work or anything that smacks of traditional labels. I am irritated when labels are thrust on me, such as when I receive mail addressed to "Mr. and Mrs. Solomont." It feels so old-fashioned. I don't want my marriage to define my identity. I worked hard in Spain to define my own role, and during that time, I learned that many other cultures conceive of life as more than simply one's occupation or relationship status. People in Spain work hard, but they also enjoy themselves while tending to their families, embarking on hobbies, traveling, and doing many other activities. My daughter Stephanie has discovered something similar while living in Colorado. As she has observed, people in the Rockies have diverse interests and passions that form integral parts of their identities. This contrasts sharply with Boston, where she and I are both reminded that, more often than not, your identity and your profession go hand in hand.

I wince in social situations when people ask me, "So what are you doing *now*?" I used to pose this question as well, back when I regarded my job as the pivotal part of my identity. Today, I respond to the question by asking, "Do you mean how do I spend my time?" While living in Spain, I used to explain that my husband was serving as ambassador, and I was doing all sorts of interesting things to support him and to make my own impact. Since returning to the United States, I do many interesting things—include my involvement on Berklee College's board of trustees and other boards, taking classes, writing, and doing consulting work—but no single activity defines me. Now I tell people, "I'm finding new ways to spend my time and discovering new meaning in my life."

In general, I orient myself toward what I call "personal growth." On my sixtieth birthday, which I celebrated shortly after our return from Spain, I made a list of sixty meaningful things I wanted to accomplish during the following year: attending lectures, learning to cook new dishes, participating in religious services, practicing meditation, losing weight, writing a children's book, and completing this book. I created a spreadsheet and, month by month, checked off items on my list. For my sixty-first birthday, I recreated my list to assign goals in four categories—body, mind, heart, and spirit. And for my sixty-second year, I'm adhering to one word: *patience*. I'm striving for patience with who I am and what I do.

Alan always promised me that when we returned from Spain, we would lead a simpler life, and today I do. Alan is still working on this. During our time in Spain, we made sure to schedule time for the two of us. Now, we find that easier. We are together more, and our time is more *relaxed*. We choose simple things to do that keep us rooted in our community. Dinners with friends, home-cooked meals, and walks in the neighborhood are activities that Alan and I find enriching.

Admittedly, the luxury of simplicity requires a degree of privilege that many people don't enjoy. And while I'm grateful for these circumstances, I also miss earning a decent salary. This sometimes bothers me, such as recently when I received a notice from the Social Security

Administration, logging all the money I've contributed over the course of my career. From 2010 to 2013, I contributed nothing financially because the State Department insisted I give up my work to go abroad. While other nations pay stipends and prescribe specific roles for diplomatic spouses, my government records a three-year gap in my work life. What my Social Security record doesn't show is that I worked hard alongside my husband and the embassy staff to make a meaningful contribution to our diplomatic mission in Spain. The injustice of this still gnaws at me to this day.

Friends often ask: "How are you feeling now? How do you top the time you spent in Spain? What did you learn?" When I arrived in Spain and struggled to find my way, I longed for the familiarity of my life in Boston. But after adjusting to living in Spain, I discovered many of the usual comforts of home right there, including community, friendship, and professional opportunities.

Reflecting back, I also recall the "pinch me" moments I experienced in Spain. Who would have imagined I'd become acquainted with Spanish royalty or that I'd meet Rafael Nadal and Antonio Banderas? Who would've predicted I'd be publicly serenaded by a group of powerful women and dear friends who were sad I was leaving, or that I'd serve as the face of my country abroad?

I also learned about the US foreign service, the sacrifice of the men and women serving in the military, and the importance of diplomacy. I ate amazing food and drank great wine, twice dining at the world's best restaurant. I danced flamenco in Sevilla and toured Gaudi's Sagrada Familia in Barcelona. I learned to live with bodyguards, footmen, a butler, and a driver. I became part of a new Jewish community. Ultimately, I fell in love with Spain, and Spain showed me a lot of love in return.

My work in Spain left me with a new sense of competence and confidence. After what I did to create and lead the women's leadership series, I know I can bring people together to create change. I feel that confidence today even when I don't quite know all the ways I might apply it. I don't know if the present period in my life will prove to be a transition between different careers, or whether I'll continue to check off disparate activities on my spreadsheet indefinitely. I do get up every day excited to see what feels right and authentic. And having the chance to feel this way—that's one of the most profound gifts my time as "the ambassador's wife" has given me.

In that spirit, I have a parting message to share: If you have the opportunity to do something different in life, something unusual and unforeseen, go for it. Take the risk, even if it feels scary or uncomfortable. These opportunities are rare, and you must seize them. Experience the unfamiliar. Strike out in a different direction. Explore a new passion. You won't regret it, no matter your age, gender, or place in life. I know I didn't.

Disfruta tu vida!

ACKNOWLEDGMENTS

S AYING THANK YOU IS A practice I value deeply. I am extremely grateful to the many people who guided me, befriended me, and helped make this book a reality. It takes a village—and in this case, a transatlantic one.

Thank you to President Barack Obama. When the White House called in early 2009 to ask Alan to serve as a United States ambassador, I had little idea what kind of journey and life-changing experience was in store for us. It was an honor to represent President Obama and to serve our country, and I'm eternally grateful for this experience.

Thank you to the United States Foreign Service Officers whose tenure at Embassy Madrid overlapped with ours. Members of our foreign service, along with others who serve our country abroad, are unsung national heroes. I was fortunate to meet Arnold and Alida Chacon, Luis and Gloria Moreno and their golden retriever Ollie, Kate Byrnes, Scott Gage, Tom and Sarah Genton, Sarah Bushore, Katie Ortiz, Terry and Leslie Vice, Stu Bailey, Jennifer Garcia, Reena Patel, Jenny Cordell, Maritheresa Frain, Ari and Monique Nathan, Susan Szmania and Dan Mangis, Syga Thomas, Scott and Christine Fagen, Kevin and Marta Hurlbert, Marc Varri, Steve and Sue Liston, Laura Smyth, Julianne and Adam Price, Kimberly Marshall, Tanya Anderson, Laura Gould, Ellen Lenny-Pessagno, and many others who serve our country with distinction and who helped me find my place at the US Embassy in Madrid.

The Spanish citizens who work at the embassy and at consular offices throughout the country are the backbone of the Embassy's diplomatic work. While members of the Foreign Service rotate to new posts every few years, the local team provides continuity, history, and devotion to a strong US–Spain relationship. Their kindness was incredible and their friendship is enduring. I am grateful to each and every member of the Madrid staff, including Kim Wise, Nancy Brown, Arancha Blanco, Aurora López de Larrinzar, Aurelio Sevillano, Rosi Smith, Irene Diaz, María José Moyano, Dr. Jose Peralba, Blanca Pardo, Ana García, Angela Turrin, Mickey Robinson, Marta Soriano, Beatriz Agenjo, Marta Peralta, Enrique Cantos, Jesús Andrés, Puchi Montes, Carmen González, Noemi Arenas, Maria Robles, Virginia Ghent, and Mauricio Sánchez. I am also thankful for the Spanish National Police officers who looked after our security and whom we knew exclusively on a first-name basis. They included Oscar, José, Goyo, Manolo, David, and María.

We were blessed to have Cristina Álvarez manage the Ambassador's Residence during our post. Cristina helped transform the residence into our home. She tended to every detail imaginable; but most importantly, she became a lifelong friend, along with her husband, Julio Carrión, and their son, Jorge.

Working at the residence with Cristina was an amazing staff that looked after us with love and constant attention. Thank you, Carlos Quelal, Ani Bóveda, Adelina Serrano, Antonio Lianes, Rosita Alvarado, Gustavo Valbuena, and Byron Chontasi. No matter what we needed, you were always there for us.

It was our great good fortune to have been embraced by Madrid's Jewish community. A special thanks to Rabbi Mario Stofenmacher, Nuria Stisin, David and Nuria Hatchwell, Monique and Maurice Hatchwell, Kareen Hatchwell, Astrid and Henry Misrahi, Karen Friedman and Javier Herreros de Tejada, Pam Rolfe, Bert and Marguerite Shader, and Al Goodman. Thank you for welcoming us into your homes and your hearts.

In addition to those I've already mentioned, Alan and I made an enormous number of good friends while we lived in Spain. There are far too many to name, but at the risk of leaving many friends out, I'd like to mention Javier Cremades and Arancha Calvo Sotelo, Ana Palacio, Antonio Garrigues, Antonio and Beatriz Oyarzabal, Maria Benjumea, Rafael Benjumea Sr., Rafael Benjumea Jr., Ann Kreis, Immaculada Pérez, Tiana del Castillo and Pedro Agustín, Placido Arango, Placido Arango Jr. and Ana María van Pallandt, Monica Oriol, Alejandro Aznar, Frank and Venturina Gelardin, Petra Mateos, Isabel and Jaime Carvajal Sr., Jaime Carvajal Jr. and Xandra Falcó, Ignacio and Teresa Galán, Rafael del Pino, Ana Romero, Wendy Wisbaum and Manolo Campa, Eva García, Astrid Gil-Casares, Bernadino and Regina León, Juan Luis Cebrian, Isabel Preysler, Antonio Camuñas, Victor Grifols, José Andres, Baroness Carmen Thyssen, Guillermo Solana, Paula Luengo, Carolina Tieu Phan, Juan Rodriguez Inciarte, Begoña Bilbao and Carlos Robles, Isabel Benjumea, and Lucia de Zavala.

The American Chamber of Commerce in Spain gave me a strong platform on which to build my work with female business leaders. Thank you to its president and our good friend Jaime Malet as well as to Aida Casamitjana and Susan Feitoza. The Women's Leadership Committee was filled with women I admire greatly, including Paloma Beamonte, Elvira Sanz, Carmen Mur, Silvia Sorribas, María Puig, Sara Blasquez, Celia de Anca, Emma Fernández, Esperanza Guisado, Isabel Tocino, Carmen Becerril, Pilar Zulueta, and Helena Herrero.

Our friends back home gave me comfort and support as we embarked on this magical adventure, and one of the delights of living in Spain was sharing our experience with visitors from home. From the time we announced we were leaving, and during every visit they made to see us, our friends brought with them the warm embrace of home. A big and grateful hug to Marsha and Tom Alperin, Sharyn Bahn, Alice Bruce, Joan and Steve Belkin, Nancy and Mark Belsky, Diane and Chester Black, Cynthia Broner, Amy Caplan and Geoff Lewis, Marci and Michael Cohen, Steve and Barbara Grossman, Nina Green, Sally Jackson, Peggy Koenig, Ronni Kotler, Win Lenihan, Lenore and Elliot Lobel, Roger Lowenstein and Judy Slovin, Jennifer Silver, and Harold and Linda Schwartz. Thank you, as well, to two special groups of visitors: a sixty-person delegation from our synagogue, Temple Beth Elohim, led by Rabbi Joel Sisenwine and Cantor Jodi Sufrin, and a Tufts University alumni group led by our dear friends President Larry and Adele Bacow. It was a privilege to share this experience in person with many of those who received my Hola letters. The letters started as a way to keep folks updated on life in Spain, and they evolved into this book. The book's title sprang from a dinner conversation with Larry and Adele where Larry suggested Lost in Spain, which evolved into *Lost and Found in Spain: Tales of an Ambassador's Wife*.

One special friend whom I miss is Peter Karoff. Peter was a friend and mentor and a great source of professional and personal support. I miss his cheerful encouragement of my work at The Philanthropic Initiative. He had urged me to write this book, and I know he would be proud of its completion.

Many people encouraged me to translate the Hola letters into a book. Among them was Helen Rees, a successful literary agent who gave me the important perspective that a collection of letters is not a book. She urged me to work with an editor who would help refine my story into something that people would read. Helen, who passed away before the book was complete, introduced me to Seth Schulman of Providence Word and Thought Company. Seth and his colleague Rachel Gostenhofer spent hundreds of hours asking probing questions and helping to shape my story into a meaningful tale. Thanks also to Helen's son Loren Rees for guiding me in the world of publishing.

Seth introduced me to Kris Pauls and the staff at Disruption Books, for which I am enormously grateful. Kris's guidance, support, and belief in this book has been extraordinary. She is a pioneer in the new publishing world and working with her has been a true pleasure.

Last, but by no means least, I want to thank my wonderful family. My mom and dad, Blanche and Len Lewis, have been great role models. From a young age, they inspired me to work for a better world. Sadly, my dad did not live to see us serve, but he would have been immensely proud of us. My mom did share this experience, and I thank her for teaching me to use the power of my voice, to be a strong woman, and to do meaningful work.

Alan's brothers and sisters-in-law Ahron and Sheera, Jay and Debra, and David and Joan all came to visit with our nieces and nephews. My sister, Beth Mendel, and her husband, Jeff, held down the family fort while we were away. They kept the family up-to-date and did the lion's share of family work while we were in Spain. Hopefully they felt our gratitude by getting to go to Ferran Adria's restaurant, El Bulli, on opening night

Alan and I are blessed to have two wonderful, beautiful, smart, and loving daughters, Becca and Stephanie. Every time they visited us in Spain, my heart sang with joy; and every time they left, I was heartbroken. Walking all over Madrid and exploring much of Spain with them was wonderfully satisfying. Part of the magic of our adventure was sharing it with our daughters, and I know they appreciated the experience as much as we did. I love them more than one can imagine and I'm proud of everything they do.

Finally, I am so grateful to Alan. He is the best ambassador and the best husband and partner one could ask for. Together, we shared the experience of a lifetime. Alan worked tirelessly to be the best ambassador he could be, working hard to forge a strong relationship with an important ally of the United States. But more important to me, he worked just as hard to ensure that our time in Spain was meaningful for both of us. Alan was my biggest cheerleader—he supported me in everything I did, and I am so appreciative of how hard he worked to make us both happy. He always said we were a partnership and that President Obama got two for the price of one. Alan is also a great editor. He edited each of my Holas, and he reviewed the entire manuscript of this book. He is the hardest working and most loving person I know. *Te quiero mucho—siempre.*

And thank you to Stella Blu, our ambassadog, who explored the streets of Madrid with me and who fell in love with Spain as much as we did.

ABOUT THE AUTHOR

S USAN LEWIS SOLOMONT HAS MORE than thirty years of experience providing strategic philanthropic counsel to private foundations. From 2010 to 2013, she served alongside her husband, Alan Solomont, in Madrid, Spain, where he was appointed as US Ambassador to Spain and Andorra under President Barack Obama. She was named International Woman of the Year by FEDEPE, the leading organization for Spanish women executives and directors. She holds a bachelor of science degree from Cornell University and a master's degree in education from Tufts University. She has two daughters, Becca and Stephanie, and a cockapoo named Stella Blu, who is the subject of her forthcoming children's book: *Stella the Ambassadog. Lost and Found in Spain: Tales of an Ambassador's Wife* is her first book.